Casebook on

Alternative 3

UFOs, Secret Societies and World Control

Jim Keith

1994
IllumiNet Press

Library of Congress Cataloging in Publication Data

Keith, Jim, 1949--
    Casebook on Alternative 3: UFOs, Secret Societies and World Control /
Jim Keith.
        p.   cm.
    ISBN: 0-9626534-9-7 : $12.95
    1. Unidentified flying object literature.
    2. Conspiracy in motion pictures.
    3. Watkins, Leslie. Alternative 3.
    4. Interplanetary voyages. I. Title II. Title: Casebook on Alternative Three.

TL789.K374   1993
303.48'3--dc20   93-32367

IllumiNet Press
Division of I-Net Group, Ltd.
P.O. Box 2808
Lilburn, GA 30226

10 9 8 7 6 5 4 3 2 1

Printed in the United States of America

With thanks to Tim Cridland

I would like to gratefully acknowledge the assistance of Vicky Bolin, X. Sharks DeSpot, Hawthorne Abendsen, Jerry Smith, Wayne Henderson, Thomas Adams, Bud McCorkle, Len Bracken, "The Franciscan," Walter Alter, Ron Bonds, Matt Love, L.A. Rollins, Thomas Lyttle, Adam Parfrey, Hatter, Raymond Nelke, Michael A. Hoffman II, David Hatcher Childress, TAL, Greg Krupey, Wes Nations, and David Crowbar.

The author is always interested in contacting individuals who have information which exposes the workings of worldwide conspiracy. I can be contacted in care of IllumiNet Press.

Contents

"I would anex the planets if I could." — **Cecil Rhodes**

"Coming events cast their shadow before. " — **Goethe**

1

The Bloody Neck!

*F*or the debunker, *Alternative 3* is a sitting duck. My first inclination, on reading the book several years ago, was to dismiss it as a poorly-done, science fictional hoax. Although widely accepted and defended among UFO buffs as an explicit revelation of the secret activities of this planet's ruling elite, watching the original British television show or reading the book based on it will quickly dispel that notion.

Intended as an April Fools' Day presentation for *Anglia TV's* usually non-fiction *Science Report* (but, because of a problem in scheduling, it is said, presented on June 20, 1977), and authored by David Ambrose and Christopher Miles, *Alternative 3* tells or, more accurately, tries to foist off a tale of scientists and 'batch consignment' commoners kidnapped to provide personnel for a project to colonize the moon and Mars — or killed to prevent the leak of information about the program. According to the teleplay and the book, our monied masters see extraterrestrial bases as the only escape from an Earth doomed by pollution and overpopulation — and they are fleeing in droves to domed cities on Mars and the moon.

'3,' they allege, is only the latest in a series of alternatives to escape a doomed Earth which have been proposed in the star chambers of the cosmic conspirators. Alternative 1, the authors would have us believe, consisted of detonating nuclear bombs in the atmosphere to allow pollution and heat to dissipate into space, whereas Alternative 2 was a plan to construct vast subterranean habitats for the elite to escape into when the going gets tough.

In a scenario worthy of an Irwin Allen disaster film, the teleplay offers film clips of British, French, Australian, Indian, and African droughts, tossing in a few earthquakes and volcanos for good measure. Tim Brinton, the show's actor-narrator, gravely intones against this cataclysmic backdrop: "The balance of the Earth's ecology was far more delicately poised than we had believed."

The text of a press release from *Anglia TV* describes the show, while not specifically revealing its fictional nature:

"A team of journalists investigating, among other topical subjects, the drought of 1976 and the changes in the world's atmospheric conditions, and also a disturbing rise in the statistics of disappearing people, follow a trail of information and scientific research through England and America.

"A Cambridge scientist and an ex-astronaut living in unpublicized retirement following a nervous breakdown, are among links in their investigation, which comes together finally in some strange discoveries about the future of life on Earth and elsewhere in the solar system.

"As a result of private screenings a few weeks ago, this programme has been acquired for simultaneous transmission in Australia, New Zealand, Canada, Denmark and Iceland and will be seen eventually in the majority of European and Asian markets.

"The programme's theme may seem extraordinary but it is scientifically possible. The question is, how far does it mirror the truth?

"With TIM BRINTON, CAROL HAZELL, SHANE RIMMER, and GREGORY MUNRO. Directed by CHRISTOPHER MILES."

The initial airing of the television show caused a public uproar in Britain, and the following day *The London Daily Mail* carried this story, headed "STAR PERFORMER."

"The director of the spoof TV documentary which portrayed life on Mars last night defended the programme after telephone calls from hundreds of angry viewers. Christopher Miles, whose *Science Report* appeared on *Anglia TV* on Monday said, 'I don't think we were irresponsible. We staged it like a documentary but the names of all the stars appeared at the end.' An *Anglia TV* spokesman added, 'We are delighted by the response. More than 10,000 people phoned in about the show.'"

The television presentation at least admits its fictional character, prominently featuring the intended date of airing, April 1, in the closing credits. Performed by actors (no debating that, they are credited in the press release and at the end of the program), the show is filled with stock disaster and NASA footage and hokey music-dubbing, including lavish dollops of Wagner's *Ride of the Valkyries* (the exception being the effective electronics of popstar-to-be Brian Eno, creating a suitably doom-portentous background, which may actually have had a lot to do with the public's horrified reaction).

Widespread public reaction was without a doubt the reason *Alternative 3* was turned into a book by Leslie Watkins and David Ambrose, published by Sphere in 1978, and this time pretending to be fact. It is upon the bare bones of the TV presentation, consisting mostly of marginally believable interviews with characters such as "Professor Gerstein," "Professor Broadbent," and the ubiquitous American astronaut "Bob Grodin," that the book is fleshed.

American astronaut "Bob Grodin" figures heavily in both the teleplay and the book, blowing the whistle on the fiendish space deception. In his disgust at the pretense he has had to maintain about *Alternative 3*, the authors have him testily say: "How they've got the bloody neck!" while pouring himself another tumbler of bourbon. When was the last time you heard an American use the expression "bloody neck"?

In another interview in the book, a drunken "Grodin" again carelessly lapses into English slang: "Let's give your pal a shout." That "interview" is composed mostly of Grodin's heavy drinking and squabbling with his girlfriend, and is obviously a set-up intended to depict Grodin's deteriorating condition, to prepare him for a literary fall. On a later visit by the television crew (omitted in the TV presentation) Grodin is found confined in a mental hospital, and later hangs himself from a "hot water pipe fixed high on the wall of his room."

Other American astronauts' tribulations and eccentricities manifesting after space flight are elaborated as more proof of a cover-up: Aldrin's depression and drinking, Irwin's becoming a Baptist minister, Mitchell's anguish after realizing that the Earth is a fragile piece of work, are offered as the guilty psychological by-products of a sinister plot. Edgar Mitchell is quoted as saying that there are three alternatives left to humankind, and that the third is "...the most viable but most difficult alternative."

The authors regale us with news stories, the majority factual but unrelated to *Alternative 3*, seemingly to intellectually lull the reader for the leap of faith it will take to buy into the abduction-to-Mars thesis. They recount the story of President Jimmy Carter toning down the tale of the UFO he saw, suggesting that he was "gotten to." They tell of the official Condon Report on UFOs "losing" some of its members (either to spontaneous combustion or to high-paying California think tanks, we are not told). Another news clipping has the Martin Marietta company building aircraft conforming to the description "flying saucers."

The disappearance of twenty people from a small coastal town in Oregon and the death of fifteen wild ponies in Dartmoor, England are mentioned, the latter an example of the cattle mutilations prevalent in the U.S., beginning in the mid-'60s. Factual CIA M-K-Ultra mind control atrocities are mulled over, but not in particular detail, and with no credible link to *Alternative 3*. Along the way the authors describe instances of Russian-American cooperation in space and offer accounts of the plight of several amnesia victims, but none of this has much to do with the core of their thesis. They seem not to care.

Gerard K. O'Neill, Princeton professor and designer of floating islands in space, is quoted as referring to his project by the name Island 3. Within 16 days after publication of this shocking indiscretion, Watkins and Ambrose inform us, a "suppression" bill is "rushed" into U.S. law so that no American scientist will make the grievous error of associating their work with the number three in future. Unbelievable "secret documents" are quoted at length in the book, without copies being reproduced, while pseudonymous witnesses reveal the neo-Orwellian horrors of *Alternative 3* by means of obviously contrived speeches and transcripts.

Alternative 3 relies heavily on the word of an alleged anonymous defector, code named "Trojan." Offering an insider's view of the conspiracy, Trojan "...wanted no money. He merely wanted to alert the public, to help stop the mass atrocities." Without Trojan, the authors maintain, "...it would have been years, possibly seven years or even longer, before ordinary people started to suspect the devastating truth about this planet on which we live."

There are long "transcripts" of the conversations of *Alternative 3* conspirators that occur in "...the wardroom of a modified Permit nuclear submarine. Thirty-five fathoms beneath ice of Arctic... No names on transcript. No names, apparently, ever used. Only nationalities and numbers. Eight Russians - listed as R ONE through to R EIGHT - and eight Americans." One submarine "transcript" is particularly transparent in its contrivance, explaining all-too-neatly the Dartmoor ponies disappearance mentioned earlier in the book, attributing it to a botched "batch consignment." Here is another typically unconvincing example of a submarine transcript, and remember, these are Americans and a Russian talking...

"R FOUR: You mean the scientific adjustments?

"A EIGHT: Yeah... the scientific adjustments... he's running off at the mouth about ethics... that sort of crap...

"A TWO: Ethics! What the hell do some of these guys think we're all at! Jesus! We're smack in the middle of the most vital exercise ever mounted... with the survival of the whole human race swinging on it... and they bleat about ethics...

"A EIGHT: That surgery bit... it really got to him...

"A FIVE: They should never have told him... he didn't need to know that... look, we owe Peterson... he's done good work... couldn't we just get him committed?

"A TWO: No way... much too risky... he'd squeal his bloody head off.

"A EIGHT: I endorse that. I'm sorry because I like the guy... but there's no choice. Anyone against an expediency for Peterson?... okay... that's carried... now for God's sake let's get down to the big problem... this stepping-up of the supplies-shuttle. Any word from Geneva?"

The transcript is all too pat, and all too "bloody" contrived.

In another transcript the authors repeat the tactic of proving their previous assertions by having the conspirators expound on the topic, in this case the secrecy bill and Gerard O'Neill:

"R SEVEN: But when O'Neill talked about Island 3...

"A EIGHT: Hold on... let me finish. Something is being done but it's being done as a blanket operation... Right now there's a secrecy Bill being scrambled on to the Statute Book and I promise you that'll close every worrying mouth."

Again, the authors have an American using British slang ("...being scrambled," i.e. 'hurried,' "on to the Statute Book," and "close every worrying mouth").

Transcripts, endless transcripts of telephone conversations predictably talk of "batch consignments" of mind-controlled, de-sexed slaves and "stinking atrocities" no more believably than the plotting that takes place "beneath ice of Arctic." The authors of the book do not have a feeling for realistic conversation, much less the conversations of Americans (the TV show faring somewhat better), and their method of continually shoring up the scenario with corroboration in the transcripts is only too obvious.

While Watkins and Ambrose thoughtfully exclude the leaders of the United States and Soviet Union from any complicity in "the terror and clinical cruelties which have been an integral part of the Operation, for that would make [them] directly responsible for murders and barbarous mutilations" they finger "high-level professionals... These professionals, we have now established, have been classifying people selected for the *Alternative 3* operation into two categories; those who are picked as individuals and those who merely form part of a 'batch consignment.' There have been several 'batch consignments' and it is the treatment meted out to most of these men and women which provides the greatest cause for outrage."

Finally we know the truth about the mysterious Men In Black who have supposedly dogged the heels of witnesses to UFOs since at least the middle of this century. They're actually dreaded "high-level professionals."

A considerable portion of the book is devoted to alleged attempts to suppress the television show. "Chris Clements," crack boy reporter for "Sceptre TV," researches the *Alternative 3* plot and ends up getting flak from various station executives. Actually, this may be one of the factual portions of the book that Watkins has referred to in correspondence. Considering the nature of the show, I can understand station execs not wanting to have anything at all to do with it. The authors present examples of office wrangling as proof of a cover-up, but my guess is that if studio or station executives did object to the program it was simply because they thought it hare-brained and a dangerous prank.

Ambrose and Watkins say that, "Many Acts of Expediency are believed to have been ordered by the sixteen men, official representatives of the Pentagon and the Kremlin, who comprise the Policy Committee [of *Alternative 3*]. Grotesque and apparently inexplicable slayings in various parts of the world - in Germany and Japan, Britain and Australia - are alleged to have been sanctioned by them. We have not been able to substantiate these suspicions and allegations so we merely record that an unknown number of people... have been executed because of this astonishing agreement between the super-powers."

While they are unable to "substantiate" these suspicions, they are able to insist that they are true.

The single impressive segment in the television show is the "suppressed" videotape of a NASA secret landing on Mars. The segment is extremely well produced (even if the occasional burst of "static" looks like it was spliced into the film, rather than actual transmission interference). The whole fly-by and landing take perhaps thirty seconds, with the landing craft fortuitously setting down so that the camera exactly captures in its frame some sort of Martian lifeform (so we are told) wriggling just beneath the red soil. In comparison, how likely is it that a camera plonked at random on a teeming Earth would capture an animal in its sights? Beautifully done, but still fake.

In summary, *Alternative 3* is a teleplay and a book which utterly lack substantiation, and the book in particular is written in a style identical to the *Weekly World News* of "Two-Headed Space Alien Gives Birth to Elvis' Lovechild" fame. What propels *Alternative 3* along in the manner of a 1940s *Amazing Stories* extravaganza set in the vicinity of Fleet Street are the "secret documents," the interviews with persons who may or may not exist and, more than that, the word of the authors who, while repeatedly maintaining "We are only interested in facts," write a television show and book loaded with as many questionable conclusions as the latest Brad Steiger UFO masterpiece.

From the first minute of the television show and the first page of the book it is the authors creating the Mars conspiracy from whole cloth (for all we can tell), weaving their story between film clips or news clippings that have almost nothing to do with their conclusions, hoked-up interviews with actors pretending to be crotchety scientists and, in the case of the book, obviously phony "secret" transcripts and documents.

It is Miles, Watkins and Ambrose who, on their word and their word alone, create and develop the *Alternative 3* mythos with almost no reference to what I laughingly refer to as facts. All the references to flights to Mars, "batch consignments"<$Ibatch consignments and so forth are found in the poorly rendered and unbelievable "secret transcripts" or created from thin Martian air by the authors.

What *Alternative 3* entirely lacks is a single piece of evidence proving the conspiracy. There is a large body of vaguely related, false, and obviously trumped-up material, but the authors omit the detail of corroborating facts in their fervent and oft-expressed quest for "facts."

Odd, but the creators of *Alternative 3*, both the book and the television show, seem not to have much cared whether anyone believed them. Apparently they thought that if they repeatedly insisted that their statements were not fictional, if they "proved" phony transcripts with other phony transcripts, that the public, that befuddled, slight-attentioned creature, would buy their story, lock, stock, and "batch consignment."

Watkins and Ambrose (particularly in the book, which omits the April Fools Day significance of the television presentation) seem to say they don't need credibility. Did Richard Shaver and his Deros have credibility? Does William Cooper? Does the White House?

There is only one problem. While perfectly secure in my knowledge that the TV show and the book are basically yellow journalism using scare tactics to make a pound, I am a little shocked to realize that, at most levels anyway, the revelations of *Alternative 3* are also true.

Deceased conspiracy researcher Mae Brussell offered her opinion about the book in her weekly radio show of June 22, 1979:

"Now the thing about... *Alternative 3* is that I've received many manuscripts and books from listeners throughout the years... but I can't remember in 15 years ever having a reaction... This book made me nauseous and I wanted to vomit, and I wanted to faint. I wanted to cry, I wanted to bang the walls down, I literally had the shakes for about a week. It was so scary because it just could be the bottom line of these conspiracies. I believe it probably is the most important book I've read in many, many years... I don't have any doubt in my mind that this is a very dangerous document to have, probably the most dangerous thing which I possess in my library at this point, and the only thing that will relieve the danger is to share it and disseminate the information... It's the one book that puts into focus all the books and articles which I have received for the last fifteen years."

Something close to the truth may have been told by the co-author of the book *Alternative 3*, Leslie Watkins, in undated correspondence. He was contacted by an American researcher who had earlier been informed by a senior editor at Penguin Books that *Alternative 3* was fiction based on fact. Watkins explained:

"The correct description of *Alternative 3* was given to you by the representative from Penguin Books. The book is based on fact, but uses that fact as a launchpad for a HIGH DIVE INTO FICTION. In answer to your specific questions:

"1) There is no astronaut named Grodin.

"2) There is no Sceptre Television and the reporter Benson is also fictional.

"3) There is no Dr. Gerstein.

"4) Yes, a 'documentary' was televised in June 1977 on *Anglia Television*, which went out to the entire national network in Britain. It was called *Alternative 3* and was written by David Ambrose and produced by Christopher Miles (whose names were on the book for contractual reasons). This original TV version, which I EXPANDED IMMENSELY for the book, was ACTUALLY A HOAX which had been scheduled for transmission on April Fools' Day. Because of certain problems in finding the right network slot, the transmission was delayed.

"The TV program did cause a tremendous uproar because viewers refused to believe it was fiction. I initially took the view that the basic premise was so way-out, particularly the way I aimed to present it in the book, that no one would regard it as non-fiction. Immediately after publication, I realized I was totally wrong. In fact, the amazing mountains of letters from virtually all parts of the world--including vast numbers from highly intelligent people in positions of authority--convinced me that I had ACCIDENTALLY trespassed into a range of top-secret truths.

"Documentary evidence provided by many of these correspondents decided me to write a serious and COMPLETELY NON-FICTION sequel. Unfortunately, a chest containing the bulk of the letters was among the items which were mysteriously LOST IN TRANSIT some four years later when I moved from London, England, to Sydney, Australia, before I moved on to settle in New Zealand. For some time after *Alternative 3* was originally published, I have reason to suppose that my home telephone was being tapped and my contacts who were experienced in such matters were convinced that certain intelligence agencies considered that I probably knew too much.

"So, summing up, the book is FICTION BASED ON FACT. But I now feel that I inadvertently got VERY CLOSE TO A SECRET TRUTH."

2

The End

*A*lternative 3 is right about one thing. Smart money is on the end of the world.

The authors attempt to convince us that escape from the Earth was the final option selected by the conspirators in Geneva once they realized the planet would soon be uninhabitable because of humanity's excesses. The Greenhouse Effect and human overpopulation are the specific dangers mentioned in *Alternative 3*, although of course there are factually no shortage of threats to human survival, many perhaps not conceived by the authors in the 1970s. Over the past two hundred years rampant industrialization and consumption of the Earth have resulted in, among other effects, the discharging of an estimated 200 billion tons of carbonized waste, carbon dioxide, chlorofluorocarbons (CFCs) and methane gases into the Earth's atmosphere, which has in turn trapped heat from the sun in much the same fashion as a greenhouse. This has caused temperatures to rise worldwide and, with geometric increases in levels of pollution, to continue to rise.

An estimation of carbon dioxide levels in the atmosphere shows approximately 288 parts per million in 1750, rising to 346 ppm as of 1990, with a probable doubling from current levels occurring by 2030, according to the *Journal of Geophysical Research*. Atmospheric carbon dioxide has increased ten percent in the last thirty years alone, and no credible solution to the problem of the Greenhouse Effect exists at this time except, perhaps, the disastrous results of the problem itself... or the third alternative.

Although no foolproof theoretical computer model of global climatic change exists, it is now widely agreed that Earth's mean temperature, stable for at least ten thousand years, is now approximately one degree Fahrenheit warmer than it was one hundred years ago. It is estimated that within one hundred years there could be enough Greenhouse gases in the atmosphere to raise temperatures worldwide by as much as seventeen degrees. Within approximately fifty years we can expect an average five-degree increase in temperature, making the climate hotter than it has been for the past four million years and perhaps triggering global changes that we can only guess at.

The Belliago Report, compiled by a group of leading climatologists in 1987, reports a probable massive death of forests worldwide by 2010, due to the inability of forests to migrate as quickly as the shifting temperature zones created by global warming. What is true of forests is also true of insects, bacteria and animals (including mankind). In addition, vast portions of arable land worldwide may in the near future become barren, causing famine on a scale never seen before.

If the migration to Mars proposed by the authors of *Alternative 3* seems an unlikely response to environmental catastrophe by the Powers That Be, there are still very likely going to be wide-scale migrations taking place, as the CIA has noted in several studies. Climatic zones may be shifting northward by 400 miles within the next 100 years, rendering vast tracts of land arid, and this will almost certainly force the migration of sizable portions of the world population, although a major change from urbanization to gathering-hunting is, I suspect, far more easily conceived than accomplished.

The picture is unrelievedly grim when it comes to curtailment of the burning of fossil fuels and reduction of carbon dioxide and fluorocarbon emissions contributing to the Greenhouse Effect. The future industrialization of the Third World dictates an almost inevitable increase in these pollutants, and a resultant rise in global temperatures. Slash and burn agriculture may also turn the Amazon rain forest into one huge cow pasture within fifty years, and the destruction of forests worldwide will only aggravate the problem of high levels of atmospheric carbon dioxide. As the trees are mowed down, they are no longer able to absorb carbon dioxide, nor are they able to produce oxygen.

Given a "reasonable" response time by governments to the problem of global warming, say fifty years to mobilize political support and to significantly reduce atmospheric emissions, we can expect a probable resultant rise of about five degrees in temperature worldwide. This level of increase in temperature has been estimated to be sufficient to melt the Western Antarctic ice sheet, causing an approximate eighteen-foot rise in sea levels worldwide. We have in fact already seen a rise in sea levels, with a recently discovered loss of forestation in Florida tentatively attributed to the effects of saltwater leaching into ground water supplies.

If all that is not enough to cause you to throw your lot in with the *Alternative 3* crowd and to immediately book passage to Mars, Earth's protective ozone layer is said to be thinning every year due to CFCs. In 1985 the British Antarctic Survey at Halley Bay stated that a huge "hole" (i.e. a 50% depletion) had developed in the ozone layer over Antarctica, and by 1987 the depletion was judged by the same team to have risen to 60%. Now ozone holes are reported over Europe and North America as well. In 1992 the ozone hole over North America extended from the Arctic to Montana, and skin cancer, caused in part by excessive exposure to solar radiation, is now the most common form of cancer in America, according to a recent report of the *American Cancer Society*. The EPA anticipates by 2050 an additional two million skin cancer cases will occur annually.

Although I cannot claim to be an expert on the Greenhouse Effect, I am able to evaluate the information that is available and to reach my own conclusions. I invite you to do the same so that you may decide whether *Alternative 3* and I share the same alarmist tendencies. My own reading and discussion of the facts cause me to reach a simple, if terribly dark conclusion. Civilization on Earth will experience massive disruption within the next 200 years, and with the proliferation of unguessed side effects of global warming (such as the propagation of disease), it is well within the realm of possibility that we will see with these events the extinction of human life on Earth.

Although not all scientists share this grim judgement on the fate of the Earth, that is beside the point, at least as regards the subject of this book. The majority who are not in the employ of major fossil fuel consuming industries seem to. It is also not inconceivable that the scientists of *Alternative 3*'s hypothetical Geneva-based conspiracy would have noted the indicators and drawn a precise conclusion.

It seems apparent that the goad for extraterrestrial migration exists. In recognition of this, have the world's elite readied or perhaps already launched their space arks? I would have to agree with *Alternative 3* that the rats who so lavishly profit from a foundering Spaceship Earth can be counted on to desert it, but as far as their identities...

3

Secret Societies
and Die Neuordning

*T*here is no question in my mind that there is a conspiracy, even a web of conspiracies running things (or attempting to run them) from the higher reaches of the global foodchain. Today, it is more a question of 'who,' rather than 'if,' and there are more than enough candidates to keep an army of muckrakers busy with their rakes for years.

In researching one begins to see the outlines of an intersection of powers implementing plans nearly identical to *Alternative 3* and, as researcher Hawthorne Abendsen points out, for these control structures "nations are merely convenient fictions."

To begin to understand what may be a real *Alternative 3* plan to lock the population of Earth into ultimate control prior to the abandonment of the planet, we need to trace a number of individuals, incidents, ideologies, and technologies, and then we will have only scratched the surface of possible connections. Nazis and the CIA; population breeding programs and American old money; slave labor camps and electronic war; NASA and Antarctic bases; these are a few of the threads in the blood-red warp.

For reasons which hopefully will become apparent, I begin the search for *Alternative 3* at what might appear to be an arbitrary moment in history; with men, most of whom died a long time ago. As we trace the actions and connections of these men, the conspiratorial web will radiate outward, and perhaps begin to take on a definite and ominous pattern.

The tale is taken up shortly after the collapse of the Third Reich, when General Reinhard Gehlen, Nazi spymaster and Knight of Malta-to-be, began negotiations with Allen Dulles and the American OSS (Office of Strategic Services). Using Nazi intelligence networks as a hole card to provide for his own survival and the survival of his huge spy network, Gehlen made a separate peace with Dulles, resulting in the clean grafting of Nazi spy apparatus to the American clandestine services. This was the birth of the CIA and part of a nexus of betrayal that continues to this day.

It is actually not so odd that Gehlen should have been able to forge ties with director Allen Dulles; Dulles' background is inextricably linked with Nazi and other elitist interests.

At the turn of the century the Dulles family, cousins of the Rockefellers, coming from a Southern slave holding background and powerful international connections, was well-connected with international banking and German interests and, when they noticed them at all, supporters of eugenics programs (i.e. selective breeding and extermination) for the lower classes. A personal philosophical statement of Allen's brother, John Foster Dulles, in 1911 illuminates the mindset and incidentally underlines a major theme of, or justification for, *Alternative 3*:

"Under natural conditions all species tend to increase with great rapidity. [After] a few generations the world would be literally crowded with life... There is a check, however... the limited capacity of the world to sustain life. As the numbers of a species increase it becomes more and more difficult for each individual to find means of sustenance... some must perish, and what is known as the law of natural selection says that the ones who will perish will be the weakest. The strongest will survive...

"With man, as with every other form of life, there is this same tendency for the birth rate to far exceed the death rate, with the inevitable result of an *overcrowded population in which some must be eliminated*. Who those eliminated are depends upon who are weakest and who are strongest in the competition which necessarily ensues.

"Biology tells us that it is only by means of this competition and elimination that progress is made. For the tendency of a race is to retrograde and *it is only by eliminating the lower members that a higher average is maintained...*" [emphases added].

Prior to World War I, The Dulles brothers were recruited into the U.S. State Department by their uncle, Secretary of State Robert Lansing. Lansing was well-connected in banking and political circles, friend to the likes of William Howard Taft, Andrew Carnegie, and Bernard Baruch. Lansing, a blatant Anglophile who took diction lessons in order to sound more British, was one of those Americans who used their power to virtually dictate to President Woodrow Wilson that the U.S. enter into an alliance with England against Germany, and supervised a steady flow of American intelligence to British spy circles.

The assassination of Archduke Ferdinand, the heir to the throne of Austria, was the match that touched off the international conflagration of World War I. Notes of the military trial examining Cabrinovic, one of the Archduke's assassins, provide clues that have been little discussed in relation to the identity of the perpetrators:

President of the military court: "Tell me something more about the motives. Did you know, before deciding to attempt the assassination, that Tankosic and Cignovic were Freemasons? Had the fact that you and they were Freemasons an influence on your resolve?"

Cabrinovic: "Yes."

The President: "Did you receive from them the mission to carry out the assassination?"

Cabrinovic: "I received from no one the mission to carry out the assassination. Freemasonry had to do with it because it strengthened my intention. In Freemasonry it is permitted to kill. Ciganovic told me that the Freemasons had condemned the Archduke Franz Ferdinand to death more than a year before."

According to the notes of the trial, Ciganovic and Tankosic held higher positions in the Freemasonic hierarchy than Cabrinovic, and Ciganovic had informed Cabrinovic that the organization had been unable to find anyone to carry out the assassination.

Count Czerin, a friend of the Archduke, relates in *Im-Welt-Krieg* that, "The Archduke knew quite well that the risk of an attempt on his life was imminent. A year before the war he informed me that the Freemasons had resolved on his death."

Why would the Freemasons have been interested in the death of Archduke Ferdinand? Far from the innocuous ritual-based men's club that they are presented as in the mainstream media, Freemasonry has long been linked to international political manipulation, and has been alleged to be a conduit for the intentions of a number of elitist interests, including the House of Rothschild and their international banking connections.

Discussing an apparent plot to involve the United States in the European war, Commander Joseph Kenworthy of British Naval intelligence reported: "The Lusitania was deliberately sent at considerably reduced speed into an area where a U-boat was known to be waiting and with her escort withdrawn."

President Wilson is known to have concealed in the archives of the Treasury Department the bill of lading of the doomed Lusitania which proved it had been carrying contraband military supplies destined for Great

Britain, putting the lie to the idea that the Lusitania was a non-military passenger vessel.

Banker Bernard Baruch controlled U.S. business during World War I as Chairman of the War Industries Board, banker Eugene Meyer headed the War Finance Corporation, while banker Paul Warburg was in charge of the Federal Reserve. All three men were agents of the Rothschild banking conglomerate.

The "War to End All Wars" devoured thirteen million souls, and at its conclusion Allen and John Foster Dulles were recruited by President Wilson's powerful advisor, banking insider "Colonel" Edward House, future architect of Roosevelt's socialist-styled "New Deal." The Dulleses travelled to Europe to attend the Paris peace conference, meeting there with members of South African diamond magnate and Freemason Cecil Rhodes' secret Round Table group, founded in 1891.

Representing the interests of British aristocracy and Rothschild-front bankers such as the Warburgs, Schroders, and Lazards, the Round Table promoted and continues to promote a New World Order based on Freemasonic/Illuminist ideas such as those held by Rhodes' mentor, John Ruskin. Ruskin in his turn is said to have been influenced by Bavarian Illuminatus Adam Weishaupt and the Isis-occultism of Edward Bulwer-Lytton, the basis of the Scottish Rite of Freemasonry, the Theosophy of Madame Blavatsky's Isis Unveiled, the Isis-Urania Temple of Hermetic Students of the Golden Dawn, and the German Thule group which was to launch and provide key philosophic underpinning to the career of Adolf Hitler. The Round Table advocated, in clear reflection of Illuminist ideas, (and still does) the destruction of all national sovereignties and surrender to an elitist ruling body, the prototype of the New World Order. The group was patterned, according to Rhodes, "on Masonic lines" with an inner "Circle of Initiates" including Rhodes, Lord Milner, future prime minister Arthur Balfour, and Lord Rothschild, whose banking cabal provides one of the most discernable influences upon the group.

"...There grew up in the twentieth century," Dr. Carroll Quigley says, "a power structure between London and New York which penetrated deeply into university life, the press, and the practice of foreign policy. In England the center was the Round Table group, while in the United States it was J.P. Morgan and Company or its local branches in Boston, Philadelphia, and Cleveland."

Inducted into the Round Table, the Dulles brothers became officers of the group's American branch, the Council on Foreign Relations (the British front group being the Royal Institute of International Affairs, known as "Chatham House"). Other members of the CFR-international banking axis included David Rockefeller, Averell Harriman (whose family was the creator of the Eugenics Records Office and the Eugenics Research Association, calling for fifty million Americans to be sterilized with the goal of perfecting the "Perfect Man" by 1980), the Astor family, Rothschild bankers Bernard Baruch and Paul Warburg (the latter hired by Kuhn, Loeb and Company at $500,000 per year to promote the creation of a Federal Reserve bank in the U.S.), and other prominent members of the international dollar-aristocracy.

In 1910 a secret meeting of bankers at Jekyll Island, Georgia finalized long-standing plans for the creation of a Federal central bank in America, which was to be represented to the public as "free of Wall Street or any monopolistic interest."... quite the opposite of the truth. Introduced via the Aldrich Bill, the plan for the Federal Reserve Bank was initially rejected by Congress. When it was realized that the Republicans were too closely connected with banking interests in the public mind, it was decided that the concept would have to be introduced by the Democrats, and this was done, resulting in the Federal Reserve Act of 1913.

Speaking of the actions of the Round Table and their banking sponsors in the creation of the Federal Reserve, Dr. Quigley wrote:

"The powers of financial capitalism had [a] far-reaching aim, nothing less than to create a world system of financial control in private hands able to dominate the political system of each country and the economy of the world as a whole. This system was to be controlled in a feudalistic fashion by the central banks of the world acting in concert, by secret agreements arrived at in frequent private meetings and conferences. The apex of the system was to be the Bank for International Settlements in Basel, Switzerland, a private bank owned and controlled by the world's central banks, which were themselves private corporations. Each central bank sought to dominate its government through its ability to control Treasury loans, to manipulate foreign exchanges, to influence the level of economic activity in the country, and to influence cooperative politicians by subsequent economic rewards in the business world."

The Rhodes group and its supporters were key in providing financing for the Russian revolution at the beginning of this century. As early as 1907 twenty million dollars was funnelled to Trotsky and Lenin, with additional large (but unreported) sums flowing from the bankers to the communists over the next few years.

In 1918 a group of fifteen international financiers secretly travelled to Petrograd under cover of a Red Cross mission. Delegates to the All-Russian Congress were purchased to the tune of one million dollars in support of Freemason Aleksandr Kerensky, with additional financing provided for the Provisional Government and their successors, the Bolsheviks.

It is usually assumed that capitalist and communist interests are diametrically opposed in their aims, but over the years the Round Table, the Rothschilds and their brethren have been happy to play cricket with communists of various stripe and in a wide variety of settings, from Mao's· China to Castro's Cuba, helping out with the odd multiple millions of dollars and pitting East/West interests against each other. I do not state this as an offhand condemnation of communist philosophy, but to point out the strange seeming-contradiction of international super-capitalists supporting a system which is portrayed as their mortal enemy.

Professor Stuart Crane describes the mechanism as employed by the Rothschilds during the Nineteenth Century:

"If you will look back at every war in Europe... you will see that they always ended with the establishment of a 'balance of power.' With every re-shuffling there was a balance of power in a new grouping around the House of Rothschild in England, France, or Austria. They grouped nations so that if any king got out of line a war would break out and the war would be decided by which way the financing went. Researching the debt positions of the warring nations will usually indicate who was to be punished."

By 1925 the Round Table had spread its organization, via three front groups, to twenty countries. The influence of this group and their allies has, if anything, increased over the years, and every American President since Freemason and Rothschild relative Franklin Roosevelt has drawn major portions of their cabinets from the American offshoot CFR.

The CFR's current roster of more than 2,600 members (within the far larger international alliance) includes key representatives of almost all of the major corporations, foundations, financial organizations, communications conglomerates and think tanks in the United States. At any given time approximately half of the CFR are serving or have served in the U.S. government. All three media-acknowledged candidates for the 1992 presidential race were linked to the CFR, while the major "non-establishment" candidate, Bo Gritz, tipped his hand to journalist Jay Katz when he slipped him a Freemasonic handshake at a survivalist convention.

Allen Dulles' star only continued to rise when, in 1920, he was appointed First Secretary of the American Embassy in Berlin. During the same period John Foster Dulles represented the international bankers in Germany, via the Bank of England and J.P. Morgan institutions. This was a time of intensive behind-the-scenes activity by British and American clandestine services in the promotion of Hitler and National Socialism, in itself a front for the occultist Thule Bund, to the fore in Germany. Thule and the associated Vril Society, were fraternally linked to English secret societies and (coincidentally?) based at least in part upon the writings of Freemason Edward Bulwer-Lytton, author of *Vril: The Power of the Coming Race*, the same man whose philosophy had fired John Ruskin and through him, Cecil Rhodes.

On March 20, 1922, banker Hjalmar Schacht (later to hold the purse strings of the Third Reich as Finance Minister, and whose father had been co-director of the German branch of Equitable Life Assurance, owned by J.P. Morgan, a Rothschild confrere), sent his friend John Foster Dulles a proposal for Germany to receive a five billion mark loan to be turned over to the central Reichsbank, thence turned over to newly-created German companies, with the stated purpose of making German war reparations possible. This was one reason that Hitler, despite his anti-Semitism, had a degree of popularity with the international bankers: he had promised to repay German war debt "to the last pfennig." In addition to arranging funding for Germany, Dulles believed that, contrary to the dictates of the Allies, the country should be re-armed, and arranged covert munitions shipments through du Pont, clients of his law firm, Sullivan and Cromwell.

Over the next few years banker Schact oversaw the entwining of German interests into massive international cartels, the most famous being the alliance of I.G. Farben chemicals with the Rockefeller's Standard Oil of New Jersey (i.e. Exxon), the formation of which included a $30 million grant from the Rockefellers. The U.S. War Department was later to state: "Without I.G.'s immense productive facilities, its intense research, and vast international affiliations, Germany's prosecution of the war would have been unthinkable and impossible..." An examination of the sources of funding for I.G. would have been more to the point. By 1929 industry in Germany had been built up so that it was second only to the United States.

John Foster Dulles was elevated to the head of Sullivan and Cromwell, the legal firm representing the German cartels, and during 1934-35 his letters to German clients bore the jaunty salutation: "Heil Hitler!" Clients of Sullivan and Cromwell included I.G. Farben (which ran the slave factory at Auschwitz), major Hitler backer Fritz Thyssen (who was to introduce Allen Dulles to Hitler), Gestapo General Kurt Von Schroeder and the Anglo-German Schroeder Bank, General Motors of Germany and other companies central to Germany's World War II effort. After the rise of Hitler's *Neuordnung* (the New Order), Dulles, representing banks and investment firms in the Rothschild/Round Table alliance, travelled to Germany to negotiate further American funding for *der Fuhrer*. During this period Mussolini's failing dictatorship was bailed out by loans from J.P. Morgan.

As far as Freemasonic President Franklin Roosevelt's allegiance, he drew much of his cabinet from the CFR, while his son-in-law, Curtis Dall, has stated succinctly what can be confirmed from numerous sources:

"For a long time I felt that FDR had developed many thoughts and ideas that were his own to benefit this country, the U.S.A. But, he didn't. Most of his thoughts, his political 'ammunition,' as it were, were carefully manufactured for him in advance by the CFR-One World Money group. Brilliantly, with great gusto, like a fine piece of artillery, he exploded that prepared 'ammunition' in the middle of an unsuspecting target, the American people — and thus paid off and retained his internationalist political support."

While Roosevelt was campaigning on promises to steer America clear of the war in Europe, numerous proofs including secret correspondence with fellow Freemason Winston Churchill show he was intent on leading the U.S. into the conflict at a gallop — significantly, from behind a desk. 83% of Americans opposed American intervention, but the bankers and Roosevelt knew better. They had other plans, including loans in excess of two billion dollars to Great Britain, the shipping of fifty destroyers and hundreds of millions of rounds of ammunition, and the training of British fighter pilots in the U.S. All German consulates were closed in this country, while U.S. ships depth charged German U-boats, still without declaration of war.

Churchill reported in secret that FDR "...said he would wage war, but not declare it [and] that he would become more and more provocative... Everything was being done to force an 'incident' that could lead U.S. to war."

Henry Stimson, founding CFR member, U.S. War Secretary, and leader of a powerful American interventionist coalition, made the following notation in his diary after a meeting with Roosevelt: "We face the delicate question of diplomatic fencing to be done so as to be sure Japan is put into the wrong and makes the first bad move — overt move."

The CFR's War and Peace Studies Project was quick with the solution to the quandary. A memorandum was sent to Roosevelt, recommending aid to China and a trade embargo on Japan, advice which Roosevelt followed. Japan's assets in the U.S. were frozen, and the Panama Canal was closed to Japanese shipping, effectively creating a stranglehold on Japanese trade.

The CFR's War and Peace Studies Project was to be a central determinant of future aims of the United States. Closely collaborating with the State Department, the Studies Project divided the world into blocs, compiling available statistics on commodities production and trade. Determining that the self-sufficient capacity of Germany and Europe was higher than that of the Western Hemisphere, the Studies Project decided that the defeat of Germany and world domination by America was the only solution. America must broaden its imperialistic aims, creating an expanding capitalist world economy and international hegemony for the U.S. It was not explicitly stated which groups or individuals would rule the U.S. during this period of expansion, although it is certain that Will Rogers was at no time under consideration.

The "foremost requirement of the United States in a world in which it proposes to hold unquestioned power," the Studies Project reported, "is the rapid fulfillment of a program of complete re-armament." Herein the course for World War II and postwar world domination by "America" was charted.

Much has been written in recent years about Roosevelt's prior knowledge of an attack on Pearl Harbor, which included American maneuvers against Japan making reprisal almost inevitable, and information of a probable attack reaching Roosevelt through at least eight different sources. It was a day of infamy, as John Toland has reiterated in his book of the same title, and Roosevelt had provoked his desired "incident."

After the attack on Pearl Harbor, Allen Dulles joined the staff of the Office of Coordinator of Information (OCI), precursor to the Office of Strategic Services (OSS). J. Edgar Hoover objected to the men Dulles was hiring, characterizing the Dulles family as "internationalists." Hoover may have been onto something.

It was strictly "business as usual" during the Second World War for many of these same "internationalists." During 1942 Standard Oil of New Jersey shipped oil to the Germans through neutral Switzerland, while General Motors equipped both sides during the conflict. The Paris branch of Chase Bank conducted millions of dollars of business with the Nazis with the approval of the central Manhattan branch, while Colonel Sosthenes Behn, the head of ITT, consulted with Hitler on communication systems and robot bombs. Ball bearings, in short supply among the allies, were shipped to Nazi-connected firms in South America by the Vice Chairman of the American War Productions Board, in partnership with Nazi Goering's cousin in Philadelphia.

An American alliance with Stalin provided tacit approval to his slaughter of six million Ukrainians during 1932-33, along with the joint German-Russian invasion of Poland, and the Russian invasion of Finland, Latvia, Estonia, and Luthuania. Eleven billion dollars in lend-lease aid was given to the USSR, along with blueprints for the atomic bomb and shipments of refined uranium, proffered by the CFR's Harry Hopkins, according to G.R. Jordan's *From Major Jordan's Diaries*. After the war the American military cooperated in Operation Keelhaul, sending two million fleeing Russians back to Russia in boxcars to face Stalin's murderous reprisals.

World War II is the story of the death of thirty-five million patriotic, slogan-shouting serfs, while billions of dollars lined the pockets of the international bankers and their cohorts, the politicians and the weapons manufacturers.

At the close of the war, so goes the standard line, Hitler committed suicide in his bunker. For my part, I am not convinced. Many other prominent Nazis escaped to conspire another day; why not Hitler, who had the entire resources of the Third Reich at his command? Hitler's notoriety dictated that his death be faked (as the deaths of other Nazis have been faked since the end of the war; Martin Bormann's six times, for instance), but the mysterious circumstances and lack of evidence of his death weigh in favor of the theory that Hitler escaped.

Wayne Henderson, in an unpublished article, offers revisionist information on Hitler's death:

"In February of 1973, a journalist was given a rare interview with a man long thought dead. Though he was generally believed to have died trying to escape Berlin - scant yards ahead of Russian troops then taking the city - Martin Bormann, close intimate of Adolf Hitler, was living in seclusion, ill, in a Redemptorist convent near Tupiza, Bolivia. He, among others, had been the recipient of a joint gift of 'Wild Bill' Donovan of the OSS (later the CIA) and certain well-controlled factions of the Vatican Elite.

"Bormann had been among the Chosen Few present at the bunker on 30 April, 1945 - others present included Otto Gunsche (Hitler's adjutant), Heinz Linge (Hitler's valet), and Julius Schaub, a trusted friend of the Fuhrer who was charged with the responsibility of destroying the files; it goes without saying that Hitler and his bride of 24 hours, Eva Braun, were also there. According to the official version, Adolf & Eva died that day, though there is some disagreement as to whether they used pistols or poison.

"What really happened on 30 April 1945, however, would seem to be quite different from the official version. Hans Bauer, the Nazi flying ace - easily one of the greatest aviators the world has yet seen - had been landing and taking off outside the Chancellory, on the Wilhelmstrasse. He had ferried the favored few in and out of Berlin, and could easily have removed Hitler and his retinue at any time, every bit as easily as he'd flown the various caches of personal wealth entrusted to him by the Nazi elite to various safe hiding-places. Indeed, Bormann and others had advised Hitler to fly to Berchtesgaden, where the faithful troops could guard them in the near impenetrable Alps.

"However, a flight - at least from the Chancellory - was unnecessary. When the Soviets took the wreckage of the bunker, they found '...behind the bookcase in Hitler's personal room... a thin, concrete, removable panel. Behind it was a man-size hole leading to a... concrete shelter far underground and 500 meters away. Another tunnel connected the shelter with an underground trolley line...' The searchers also found 'a charred note in a woman's handwriting... (telling) her parents not to worry if they did not hear from her in a long while.' The Hitlers need not have taken the trolley very far, either, as Bauer could easily have picked them up at a safer airstrip than Wilhelmstrasse and flown them to any destination within fuel range. The body later identified - in the official version - as that of Hitler was more likely (considering the fact that the dentition of the corpse and that reflected in Hitler's dental charts don't match) that of Julius Schreck, a longtime fanatical supporter of the Fuhrer and Hitler's personal driver; Schreck is known to have resembled Hitler so closely that he often acted as his boss' 'double,' and Schreck's 'death' (in a poorly-staged and undocumented auto accident in 1936) made it that much easier for the devotee to take the place of his master among the charred remains of the Chancellory. Would Schreck willingly allow himself to become the corpse at Berlin? Fanatics and zealots have been known to do much stranger things."

Henderson's account is corroborated by another statement of the Russians in September of 1945: "No trace of the bodies of Hitler or Eva Braun has been discovered... It is established that Hitler, by means of false testimony, sought to hide his traces. Irrefutable proof exists that a small airplane left the Tiergarten at dawn on April 30 flying in the direction of Hamburg. Three men and a woman are known to have been on board. It has also been established that a large submarine left Hamburg before the arrival of the British forces. Mysterious persons were on board the submarine, among them a woman."

Henderson describes the fate of Rudolph Hess, "...the man who did more to set up the U.S./Vatican/Nazi connection than anyone else; he vanished into the waiting arms of the Masonic Lodges in England, long pro-Fascist and thick as thieves with their continental counterparts, Thule and the Teutonic Knights among them, on the night of 10 May 1941; the double who later served his prison sentence at Spandau and died silent in 1987 fooled only the most casual observers."

Again in support of Henderson's account, I have found that the psychiatrist chosen to examine Hess was Dr. Ewen Cameron, the soon-to-be-infamous CIA mind control doctor whose activities will be considered later in this book. Cameron reported that Allen Dulles confided to him that the captive in Spandau prison was not the real Hess, but an imposter. Hess, so

Dulles explained, had been executed on the orders of Winston Churchill. Attempting a positive identification of Hess by physically locating a World War I chest wound, Cameron was prevented by guards from doing so.

There has been much speculation about Nazis setting up a secret Antarctic base after the war, with Hitler possibly present, however it is just that — speculation — so far as I can determine. While there was a lot of Nazi submarine and tanker activity in the vicinity of Antarctica during this period, and a search for Germans mounted by the Americans utilizing 4,000 troops (suggesting the Allies definitely thought something was going on down there), nothing other than circumstantial evidence and hearsay suggests a German South Polar base was actually established. There is the possibility that the Antarctic was used as a stopping-off base for escaping Nazis, but evidence suggests that those who were able to escape Nuremberg eventually went elsewhere, although probably not to the moon or Mars.

4

The Fourth Reich

At the end of World War II Martin Bormann, Deputy Fuhrer and head of the Nazi party, and Hermann Schmitz, chief executive of I.G. Farben, hatched a plan for the continuance of Nazi goals not to be limited by territorial and national boundaries. Bormann, anticipating the destruction of the Third Reich, worked out the logistics for the escape from Germany of an estimated 10,000 prominent Nazis, using huge caches of Nazi loot as funding. These were reported to consist of in excess of ninety-five tons of gold, tons of other precious metals and jewels, and billions of dollars in currency, both real and counterfeit. Other stockpiled Nazi resources were tonnages of specialty steel, industrial machinery, and secret blueprints that could be used in the domination of areas of post-war manufacturing. These plans almost surely included the Trojan horse-style grafting of Nazi intelligence onto the OSS by SS General Reinhard Gehlen and Allen Dulles.

The Research and Analysis branch of the OSS observed in 1945 that:

"The Nazi regime in Germany has developed well-arranged plans for the perpetuation of Nazi doctrines after the war. Some of these plans have already been put into operation and others are ready to be launched on a widespread scale immediately upon termination of hostilities in Europe."

Summarizing these plans, the OSS group said, "Nazi party members, German industrialists and the German military, realizing that victory can no longer be attained, are now developing postwar commercial projects, endeavoring to renew and cement friendships in foreign commercial circles and planning for renewals of pre-war cartel agreements.

"German technicians, cultural experts and undercover agents have welllaid plans to infiltrate into foreign countries with the object of developing economic, cultural and political ties. German technicians and scientific research experts will be made available at low cost to industrial firms and technical schools in foreign countries. German capital and plans for the construction of ultra-modern technical schools and research laboratories will be offered at extremely favorable terms since they will afford the Germans an excellent opportunity to design and perfect new weapons."

A secret meeting was convened between Bormann and prominent German industrialists on August 10, 1944 in Strasbourg. The minutes of the meeting state:

"The [Nazi] Party is ready to supply large amounts of money to those industrialists who contribute to the post-war organization abroad. In return, the Party demands all financial reserves which have already been transferred abroad or may be later transferred, so that after the defeat a strong new Reich can be built."

Reichsbanker Hjalmar Schact managed the relicensing and relocation of approximately 750 German companies outside of the country, while Otto Skorzeny, Hitler's "favorite commando" and leader of the Werewolf units, collaborated with Bormann (as well as the Vatican and, according to the Vatican Press Office, the Freemasons) in creating the Nazi "rat lines." These were escape routes to transport prominent Nazis out of Germany which included, it is said, 20,000 safe houses in Switzerland alone.

The Nazis collaborated in the formation of the *Odessa* (an acronym for "Organization of Veterans of the SS"), and its sister organization *Die Spinne* (The Spider), organizations intended to establish colonies of Nazis worldwide, and in the launching of offshoot groups, utilizing in part the resources of an estimated 200,000 foreign members of the SS. Other organizations under the *Odessa* umbrella were the *Consortium*, managing *Odessa* finances from Lima, Peru and run by Klaus Barbie and other war criminals, with *SA Estrella* in Ecuador, managing Bormann's personal finances and run by SS man Alfons Sassen.

Bormann is said to have escaped to *Kolonie Waldner 555*, a forty-by-one-hundred mile Nazi fortress on the Brazil-Paraguay border, linked with fourteen other such fortresses in the same area. Other touch-down points for escaping Nazis included the United States, South Africa, South America, Egypt, Spain, Canada and Indonesia.

War criminals Klaus Barbie and Friederich Schwend set up escape routes to South America for their compatriots, while simultaneously being in the paid employ of U.S. Army Counterintelligence (CIC). Evidence shows that Barbie went to Bolivia, Schwend to Peru, Walter Rauff to Chile, Alfons Sassen to Ecuador, Otto Skorzeny, Hans-Ulrich Rudel and Heinrich Muller to Argentina, while Josef Mengele escaped to Paraguay. Maintaining close ties to each other and other escaped Nazis, this network evolved into what has been termed the Nazi International, run by Otto Skorzeny and headquartered in Madrid. The Nazi International would be key in the establishment of worldwide arms, terrorist, and drug trafficking networks, although these crimes perhaps pale in comparison with the subversion of American intelligence, in collaboration with Allen Dulles, the result of which may be said to have been the creation of the Cold War and the continuing destruction of democracy in America.

Reinhard Gehlen, said to have been setting up Nazi Werewolf resistance groups at the end of the war, collaborated with OSS director Allen Dulles in combining Nazi and American intelligence apparatus. Gehlen has said that a "gentlemen's agreement" existed with Dulles "for a number of reasons never set down in black and white... Such was the element of trust that had been built up between the two sides during this year of intensive personal contact that neither had the slightest hesitation in founding the entire operation on verbal agreement and a handshake."

Gehlen reminisced, "I remember the terms of the agreement well...

"1. A clandestine German intelligence organization was to be set up, using the existing potential to continue information gathering in the East just as we had been doing before. The basis for this was our common interest in a defense against communism.

"2. This German organization was to work not 'for' or 'under' the Americans, but 'jointly' with the Americans.

"3. The organization would operate exclusively under German leadership, which would receive its directives and assignments from the Americans until a new government was established in Germany.

"4. The organization was to be financed by the Americans with funds which were not to be part of the occupation costs, and in return the organization would supply all its intelligence reports to the Americans.

"5. As soon as a sovereign German government was established, that government should decide whether the organization should continue to function or not, but that until such time the care and control (later referred to as 'the trusteeship') of the organization would remain in American hands.

"6. Should the organization at any time find itself in a position where the American and German interests diverged, it was accepted that the organization would consider the interests of Germany first."

Carl Oglesby has written that, "in fact the Gehlen Org substantially pre-empted the CIA's civilian character before it was ever born. The CIA was born to be rocked in Gehlen's cradle. It remained dependent on the Org even when the Org turned into the BND [*Bundesnachrichtdienst*, the German federal intelligence service]. Thus, whatever the CIA was from the standpoint of the law, it remained from the standpoint of practical intelligence collection a front for a house of Nazi spies.

"The Org was not merely military, which is bad, not merely foreign, which is much worse, and not merely Nazi, which is intolerable; it was not even professionally committed exclusively to the security of the U.S. and Western Europe. It was committed exclusively to the security of the *Odessa*."

Military intelligence historian Colonel William Corson concurs: "Gehlen's organization was designed to protect the *Odessa* Nazis. It amounts to an exceptionally well-orchestrated diversion."

Once the Gehlen Org was in place, with an estimated 4,000 intelligence specialists in Germany and more than 4,000 undercover operatives in the Soviet bloc, the perceived threat to the United States by the Soviets was aggravated by Nazi intelligence, and the Cold War was inevitable. Gehlen and his cronies seemingly never admitted that Germany had lost the war and simply persisted with Nazi objectives, using different means to destroy the USSR, namely collaboration with the United States and the OSS/CIA. The Nazis may have, in addition, foreseen the devastating results of a Cold War between the U.S. and the USSR. The Cold War provided a financial burden which has destroyed Russia and left the United States as the world's biggest debtor nation — and a virtual colony of the original Axis powers, Japan and Germany.

After the war, the American rocket program was conceived and controlled by 600 Nazis brought to the U.S. during Dulles' Project Paperclip (a project only discontinued in 1973). In choosing German scientists to be brought into the United States, the list of candidates was compiled by Werner Osenberg, commander of the Gestapo's scientific section, now in Dulles' employ. Files incriminating German officers and scientists were reportedly destroyed or changed, and Osenberg, in charge of those files, was in a favored position for the alterations.

At the time of the immigration of the Paperclip Nazis the *Chicago Herald Tribune* pointed out that the same men "exhaustively screened" in America and proven to have held no allegiance to Hitler, had earlier been "exhaustively screened" in Germany to establish that allegiance.

German scientists entered the U.S. under highly curious conditions, and in defiance of normal immigration policies. While supposedly under the most strict of military security, custody precautions were incredibly lax, as they would remain in the years to come. Ernst Steinhoff, an official at the Peenemunde V-2 rocket base, wasn't met when his boat docked, forcing him to hitchhike to the Aberdeen Proving Ground in Maryland. At White

Sands an intelligence officer said of the transplanted Nazis, that there was "no attempt to place them in anything resembling custody."

One Nazi scientist, Rudolf Hermann, gained some notoriety at Wright Field by holding daily roll calls in a brown uniform and giving speeches to his underlings about the necessity of maintaining loyalty to Hitler.

Nazis were employed in the formation of German state security, Radio Liberty, the Voice of America, and the U.S. Army Historical Division, and were used to fill top Pentagon posts and positions in industry. Additionally, Nazi scientists were employed in Chief and Deputy positions in every major division and laboratory in the American rocket program.

Although it has been a carefully guarded secret, Nazi scientists were also involved in the Army and CIA psychochemical experiments conducted on American enlisted men at Edgewood Arsenal in Maryland, and at the Army intelligence base at Fort Holabird, Maryland: this was the beginning of the CIA's M-K-Ultra mind control experiments. Experiments in some cases copied from Dachau were performed on over seven thousand American soldiers without their consent (they were told in some cases that they would be testing "summer clothing"), in violation of guidelines set at the Nuremberg trials. Nerve gases, including the deadly Nazi chemical agents Tabun and Sarin, were tested on unwitting recruits, along with a host of psychochemicals, including LSD, some resulting in deaths and permanent crippling of enlisted men.

Among the Nazi scientists transplanted to the U.S. was SS Major Werner von Braun, factually the most decorated of the Nazi breed during World War II, and a man who had joined the SS at the behest of its chief, Heinrich Himmler. Von Braun, who was to be head of the National Aeronautics and Space Administration (NASA) and the author of a book with the sonorous title *Das Marsprojekt* (1952), was responsible for running the Peenemunde rocket base during World War II, and his brainchild, the V-2 missile, would have carried atom bombs to New York if Nazi plans had proceeded farther.

During the war German V-2s were responsible for the deaths of 7,000 British citizens, however through false reports channelled through captured *Abwehr* agents British intelligence was able to re-target the missiles from falling mostly on upper class neighborhoods into the working class neighborhoods of South London — whew!

It is estimated that 100 slave laborers died per day on average in the construction of the V-2s, with an estimated 20,000 dying during the course of the war. Policy dictated that slaves hung for punishment were left suspended for days as a reminder to the surviving unfortunates. A survivor of Peenemunde describes such an instance: "Fifty-seven were hung. An electric crane, in the tunnel, lifted twelve prisoners at a time, hands behind their backs, a piece of wood in their mouths, hanged by a length of wire attached at the back of their necks to prevent them from crying out."

Yves Beon of the French Resistance swore that, although the SS was employed to manage the slave force used in construction of rockets, they acted on the orders of von Braun and General Dornberger, although, according to both of these men, they in turn followed orders. As mentioned, it can be substantiated that von Braun attended conferences on slave labor allocations with other high-ranking SS officers, and there is no indication that he or Dornberger offered any protest about the conditions in the slave camp.

Von Braun's security record, including a statement by the military governor in occupied Germany stating that von Braun was "an ardent Nazi" and "regarded as a potential security threat," was ignored by American intelligence.

Von Braun refused to work in American rocketry unless General Walter Dornberger, his mentor at Peenemunde, was released from captivity. Dornberger, who had been convicted at Nuremberg of collaborating to murder 6,000 prisoners, and had been sentenced to be hung, received a full pardon arranged by High Commissioner John J. McCloy.

McCloy is the man who would later be president of Rockefeller's Chase Manhattan Bank, legal counsel to the "Seven Sisters" of oil, chairman of the CFR, and serve on the Warren Commission for official cover-up, along with Allen Dulles. During the period of supposed "de-Nazification" following the war, McCloy pardoned, almost to a man, the 70,000 Nazis accused of war crimes.

It should be noted that McCloy represents an interface between international banking and Nazi interests, with connections going back to after World War I, when he was a lawyer in the employ of I.G. Farben. During the 1936 Olympics in Berlin, McCloy shared a box with Hitler, and was in contact with Hess before his flight to England in 1941.

The American government has been reticent to disclose that security breaches were numerous after the Germans were brought into this country. Wright Field specialist Heinz Gartmann, said to have been negotiating with a Russian factory prior to his attempted departure from the United States, was apprehended leaving with rocket engine blueprints in his luggage, while Walter Jessel, an interrogator of the rocket scientists for the Army, claimed that there was a conspiracy between von Braun, Dornberger, and Dornberger's chief of staff to withhold information from U.S. officers.

Three German scientists were found to have illegal mail drops in El Paso, Texas where they received money and coded messages from foreign sources. Other instances of Nazi scientists receiving money from unknown sources were not investigated by the military, including an instance when one third of the German Paperclip group simultaneously bought expensive cars that they were reportedly unable to afford on their salaries. There were also repeated suspicions that rockets were being sabotaged, and that components were missing from recovered missiles.

Von Braun's brother, brought into the country apparently only because he was related to the scientist, was caught selling a bar of platinum to an El Paso jeweler. Although he was unable to explain how he came by the platinum, the Justice Department ordered that the case not be investigated.

When U.S. astronauts first landed on the moon, Jean Michel, a survivor of the Dora rocket factory, was one of the few persons to raise a critical voice. Speaking of Nazi collaboration in the creation of the U.S. space program, Michel said, "I could not watch the Apollo mission without remembering that triumphant walk was made possible by our initiation to inconceivable horror."

If one is still apt to think of von Braun and ninety of his fellows at command level in NASA as cranky eggheads and "reformed" Nazis, their connections to the assassination of John F. Kennedy should be examined.

"William Torbitt," (deceased Texas lawyer David Copeland), author of the superb *Nomenclature of an Assassination Cabal,* named von Braun, directing the Security Division of NASA, as a key operative in the Kennedy assassination. Von Braun's offices reportedly served as a meeting place for men in the higher levels of the plot hierarchy, and he was closely associated with Defense Industrial Security Command (DISC, now DISCO), the secret police agency of the monolithic American munitions manufacturers. Many of DISC's executives are reported to have been Mafia, creating a rich stew. Alleged conspirators Colonel Clay Shaw of the National Security Agency, Guy Bannister, David Ferrie, Lee Harvey Oswald, and Jack Ruby have been shown to have been in contact with, and possibly agents for DISC, while Walter Dornberger, von Braun's mentor, has also been implicated as a high level conspirator in the plot.

"Torbitt" names Lyndon Johnson and J. Edgar Hoover as heading the conspiracy, with Canadian lawyer Louis Mortimer Bloomfield as the coordinator for the operation, responsible only to Johnson and Hoover. Bloomfield was said to be in charge of the Permindex organization, an umbrella for the layers of action networks in the assassination cabal, but "Torbitt" doesn't mention that Bloomfield — Major Bloomfield — had been a longtime operative of the British Special Operations Executive, under the direction of "retired" SOE chief Sir William Stephenson (Intrepid), as well as being a member of the conspiratorial Knights of Malta — long linked to

Nazi and Fascist interests. Bloomfield was also an executive representative for the International Law Association, a legal arm of the Rhodes Round Table.

Bloomfield's immediate juniors in the conspiracy are alleged to have been Ferenc Nagy and Jean De Menil, in charge of a group of Russian, European and Middle Eastern exiles called Solidarists; Carlos Prio Soccaras, ex-Cuban President, heading a group of Cuban exiles; H.L. Hunt, in charge of a section of the American Council of Churches, an alleged front for spies; Clifford Jones, ex-lieutenant governor of Nevada, and Bobby Baker, heading an organization of Mafia and gamblers called The Syndicate; along with von Braun, in charge of the Security Division of NASA.

Hoover controlled the investigation of the JFK assassination, while familiar faces Allen Dulles and John McCloy helped determine what seems to have been the pre-arranged verdict of the Warren Commission, that Lee Harvey Oswald was the lone assassin. After the death of Jack Ruby, Associated Press' Bernard Bayzer reported that Ruby had maintained that Nazis and Fascists were behind the Kennedy assassination. A fair characterization, it seems to me.

After World War II there was a resurgence of Nazi interests in Germany. Details such as that West German Chancellor Konrad Adenauer had employed slave labor in his home and garden during the war, and that his Secretary of State, Globke, had been a top official of the Reich Office for Jewish Affairs, were overlooked, possibly because of the fact that Adenauer had been vetted and approved by Reinhard Gehlen.

By 1951 the *Bundestag* had passed a law requiring that German administrators dismissed during the Allied occupation must be reinstated, and within two years 163,577 administrators who had been employed in the Third Reich had been readmitted to government. Thus, the administrative hierarchy of the Nazis was restored.

In 1953 the British arrested a group of former Nazi officials including Dr. Werner Naumann, former State Secretary in Goebbels' Propaganda Ministry, Karl Kaufmann, ex-Gauleiter of Hamburg, SS General Paul Zimmermann, Gustav Scheel, Gauleiter of Salzburg, Austria, Dr. Heinrich Haselmeyer, head of the Nazi Student League, Dr. Karl Scharping, a propaganda official under Goebbels, and Heinz Siepen, also an ex-Gauleiter. These men were reported to be the leaders of a group of 125 important Nazis whose purpose had been "the overthrow of the Bonn parliamentary regime." Prior to his arrest Naumann had been engaged in secret conferences with Adenauer. Evidence presented to Adenauer by the British "revealed a wide-spread plot with ramifications into many political parties and other influential organizations of West Germany."

When confronted with information about the activities of Naumann and his group in attempts to revive Nazism, Bonn Justice Minister Dehler reported that, "He was trying to fill key positions in the rightist parties with his supporters. The final goal was the restoration of the Nazi dictatorship with emphasis on the German race and its leadership role. [He] plotted to destroy the democratic system in Germany with considerable support from abroad."

Adenauer requested that the Naumann proceedings be brought under German jurisdiction, which the British agreed to. At the time the Bremer *Nachrichten* reported threats by the Naumann lawyers to reveal "the true background of the case" if Naumann and his group were not released. Within three months of being transferred to German jurisdiction, the conspirators were released, and within a year and a half the court dismissed the case without trial or hearing.

Naumann and his gang seem to have succeeded in their plans. Polls show that by 1958 the German populace regarded Hitler as "the greatest statesman of all time," and that 7-8 million Germans remained dedicated to Nazism.

Kurt P. Tauber, writing in the *New York Times* magazine in 1959, stated that under Adenauer "has come the return to social, economic and political power of precisely those commercial and industrial elites who supported a megalomaniac imperialism under the Empire."

In the 1970s all 176 generals in the West German Army were veterans of service under Hitler. *The Brown Book* on Nazis reports that 1,800 major Nazis held positions in the German government or were drawing pensions on wartime service during the 1970s. Fifteen government ministers, 828 judges and judicial officials, 245 senior diplomats, and 297 police officials were reported to have been members of the Third Reich, while Nazi officers have been involved in the resurgence of Nazi youth groups in Germany.

In recent years the Nazi International has been linked to the Freemasonic "shadow government of Italy," the Propaganda Due Lodge (P2). P2 controlled large portions of European and American intelligence and banking, its expansion during the 1970s, according to Italian secret service documents, engineered by the lodge's Venerable Master and Knight of Malta Licio Gelli, with the assistance of Knight of Malta Alexander Haig (also implicated in the underground "Skorzeny File" as a member of the Nazi International) and CFR agent Henry Kissinger. Kissinger's mentor is Fritz Kraemer, a thirty year member of the Pentagon Plans Division and recently involved in promoting the Star Wars program. Kraemer was alleged by researcher Mae Brussell to have been an officer in the SS.

P2 is reported to have been responsible for the death of Pope John Paul I, thirty-three days after he assumed the papacy. David Yallop, in *In God's Name*, says that the Pope didn't die by heart attack, as was reported, but was poisoned because of his plans to expose the Freemasonic membership of high-ranking Vatican officials, and to rein in the Vatican's corrupt financial networks. He believes that P2 was controlled by some unknown higher authority, through Gelli. Swiss publications allege this to be the Freemasonic Alpina Lodge of Switzerland, with a membership including Club of Rome founder Aurelio Peccei and Henry Kissinger, although conspiratologists allege that the Freemasons have long provided a sort of underground railroad for the activities of Illuminist-banking interests allied around the House of Rothschild.

Yallop maintains of P2 that "...there are still branches functioning in Argentina, Venezuala, Paraguay, Bolivia, France, Portugal and Nicaragua. Members are also active in Switzerland and the U.S.A. P2 interlocks with the Mafia in Italy, Cuba and the U.S.A. It interlocks with a number of the military regimes of Latin America, and with a variety of groups of neo-Fascists. It also interlocks very closely with the C.I.A. It reaches right into the heart of the Vatican."

Journalist Mino Pecorelli, a P2 member, claimed that the P2 was actually run by the CIA; that is, he did until he was killed with two pistol shots to the mouth, the standard Mafia penalty for saying too much. If Pecorelli was right, another question might be asked: who runs the CIA? Evidence is heavily weighted against the American people.

Former CIA Director Stansfield Turner may have betrayed a link between the CIA and P2 when he admitted that Pope John Paul's personal physician, one of the first to examine him after his death, was a long time CIA asset.

Stephen Knight, another in a long line of journalists alleged to have died under mysterious circumstances, saw things differently. Noting that the roster of P2 implicates virtually every political group in Italy except for the communist party, and based upon information from a source in British intelligence, Knight said that Gelli was KGB, and that the P2 is only the tip of the iceberg of a worldwide penetration of Freemasonry by the KGB. According to Knight "the 'jobs for the brethren' [i.e. job favoritism for fellow Masons] aspect of... Freemasonry has been used extensively by the KGB to penetrate the most sensitive areas of authority, most spectacularly illustrated in the years since 1945 by its placing of spies at the highest levels of MI5 and MI6."

More recently Knight of Malta Ronald Reagan and his presidential successor, the scion of an international banking family, 33rd degree Mason, CIA, CFR, and Skull and Bones Society member George Bush, showed no unwillingness to collaborate with Nazis and Fascists in their numerous illegal, covert operations.

Reagan's acquaintance with Nazism goes back to the 1940s, when he was Gestapo agent Errol Flynn's roommate and visited Flynn's senior agent, Dr. Herman Erban, on several occasions. Reagan was a member of the Free Europe Committee, which included Nazis in its leadership, and his appointments secretary while Governor of California and later President of the United States was Helene von Damme, who had come to California as translator for Otto von Bolschwing and his high-tech CIA front TCI. Von Bolschwing had been a Captain in Heinrich Himmler's SS and Adolph Eichmann's superior in Europe and Palestine, and worked with Dulles' OSS, taking over a major portion of Gehlen's network in 1954.

George Bush's background is old Connecticut banking (y'all), and his father, Prescott Bush, was a member of the W.A. Harriman international banking firm, a director of the Columbia Broadcasting System, Inc., the Prudential Company of America, Union Banking Industries, Inc. and the U.S. Guaranty Trust, among other companies. While at Yale University, Prescott Bush was initiated into the secret Skull and Bones Society (whose emblem indicates a probable Freemasonic affiliation), as George was later to be, and was part of the British/CFR/Rothschild banking clique instrumental in financing the rise of the Hitler and the Russian communists.

When six Fascists were noted on George Bush's campaign staff in 1988, he quickly made the roster of his "ethnic outreach" group unavailable. The staff included Florian Galdau of the still-existing Romanian Iron Guard, a group formed by the SS, Philip Guarino of the Freemasonic P2 Lodge, and Nicolas Nazarenko, of the German SS Cossack Division. Other members were Laszlo Pasztor, Nazi collaborator and member of the SS's Arrow Cross party, and Radi Slavoff, member of a Bulgarian cell formed by the Nazi Bulgarian Legion. Co-chairman Jerome Brentar admits to having assisted hundreds of Nazis to emigrate to the United States.

An examination of the activities of the CIA during the time when George Bush was director provides a clear sense of the identity of international conspiracy. During this period we see the CIA closely linked to the drug, arms smuggling, and assassination networks of the Nazi "Iron Circle" of police and intelligence agencies in South America, and, particularly through the activities of the CIA's JM Wave office in Miami, to the umbrella of Skorzeny's Nazi International and its worldwide network of collaborators. In this milieu, which was connected to and spawned such operations as Bay of Pigs, the Kennedy Assassination, and Iran-Contra, Nazi International agents such as Frank Bender (allegedly aka Fritz Sven) and American-Chilean DINA agent Michael Townley worked hand-in-glove with American CIA agents to promote agendas designed to undermine American and world democracy.

In retrospect, it would be a mistake to see the grafting of German spydom and the Nazi International onto American intelligence as an entirely alien "virus" contaminating the morality and lofty purposes of the American establishment. As can be seen by the activities of U.S. and British business, statecraft, occult groups, and "aristocracy" in their role in promoting Hitler to power, and the orientation and alliances of such men as the Dulles brothers and the world-spanning banking and industrialist alliances they represented, the Nazis were no isolated phenomenon, only one expression of a multi-faceted and murderous worldwide game.

Technology is a means for achieving a purpose, a will to power, and when German technology was transferred to the United States and other countries after World War II, it was marshalled, hoarded even as it was being shared. The controlling reins of German technologies such as rockets, advanced aircraft, computers, and atomics were never fully surrendered; inner circle control, through knowledge obtainable only in the inner circle, was retained by Nazis and their sympathizers.

While thousands of Nazis were incorporated into the government, industry, and intelligence agencies of the United States, the public relations image of men like Mengele, Bormann, and Hess could never have been rehabilitated in the mind of a public who had fought a devastating war against them. These men were forced to function behind the scenes from such localities as South America, Spain, Egypt and South Africa, fully linked via the Nazi International and its intermediaries with world events as they unfolded, but unable to show their faces.

It is in this environment of extensive collaboration and infiltration by Nazis and Fascists, a collaboration that involves a long-term continuance of Nazi goals separated from earlier German territorial goals, and an overall shepherding and betrayal by international monied interests, government and intelligence agencies, that America's descent into totalitarianism, genocide and mind control becomes understandable, and the *Alternative 3* template first becomes visible.

5

UFOs and the Secret Space Program

*T*he book *Alternative 3* maintains there is "abundant evidence that by 1951 the super-powers were far more advanced in space technology than they have ever admitted" and in this it is correct. There is a strong case to be made for UFOs as part of hidden and high echelon government projects, utilizing the secrets of flying disk craft received from the Nazis at the end of World War II. The timeline certainly fits.

In the *South Wales Argus* for December 13, 1944, Marshall Yarrow of Reuters stated: "The Germans have produced a 'secret' weapon in keeping with the Christmas season. The new device, which is apparently an air defense weapon, resembles the glass balls which adorn Christmas trees. They have been seen hanging in the air over German territory, sometimes singly, sometimes in clusters. They are colored silver and are apparently transparent."

These were the famous "Foo Fighter" balls (from the French *feu*, fire) which accompanied and, it was reported, destroyed some incoming Allied fighter missions during the latter days of the war. In discussions of UFO phenomena by the military their existence is invariably ignored.

Renato Vesco, writing in *Intercept — But Don't Shoot* says that the Foo Fighters were real, termed *Feuerballs* (fireballs) by the Germans, and constructed at Wiener Neustadt. They were supposedly the technological basis for the much larger German *Kugelblitz* (Ball Lightning Fighter), with a design conforming to popular concepts of "flying saucers." These designs have been attributed to German scientists Habermohl, Miethe, and

Schriever, and the Italian physicist Bellonzo. Based upon an article in the October 15, 1954 edition of the French newspaper *Le Lorrain*, one saucer construction site, from which a disk took off on February 14, 1945, was Prague, Czechoslovakia; another construction site was located at Breslau, Germany.

After the war, Habermohl is said to have gone to the Soviet Union, while Miethe went to the United States and worked at the A.V. Roe company in Canada on the Avro flying disk craft, while Schriever stayed in Germany, to die in Breslau in 1953.

Flugkapitan Rudolph Schriever said that in 1941 he had designed a prototype "flying top," and that the craft had been in the testing stages in 1945, but with the advance of the Allies the prototype had been destroyed. He maintained until his death that the various UFO reports since the end of the war showed that his *Kugelblitz* designs had been discovered and put into production.

A confidential Italian document, obtained by the OSS from an informer in Switzerland, stated that during the latter part of the war the informer had observed an encounter between an unknown craft and Allied planes: "A strange flying machine, hemispherical or at any rate circular in shape, attacked them at a fantastic speed, destroying them in a few seconds without using any guns."

Another German researcher into flying disk craft during World War II was Victor Schauberger. Designs of his "Flying Hat" aircraft show that they were similar in configuration to many of the saucers reported since the late 1940s, particularly the bell-shaped variety popularized by photos taken by outer space gadabout George Adamski. Schauberger, whose researches were classified high priority by the German government, was researching "...not nuclear fission, but nuclear fusion" and had apparently achieved several working models of his disk craft. Schauberger travelled to the United States after the war and then, one day in Chicago in the early fifties in a foreshadowing of *Alternative 3's* missing scientists theme, "just vanished."

There were numerous reports of "flying saucers" travelling singly or in formation in the vicinity of the Canadian border in 1947. At about this time, a report from the Canadian government said, "The Defense authorities are examining all ideas, even revolutionary ones, that have been suggested for the development of new types of supersonic aircraft, also including flying disks. This, however, is still in the beginning phase of research and it will be a number of months before we are able to reach anything positive and seven or more years before we come to actual production."

The Canadians were protesting too much. Visiting the aircraft plant of Avro Canada Ltd.Avro Canada Ltd. in 1953, John B. Macauley, assistant secretary of the American Defense Department, got a look at a functional flying saucer. "I've never seen anything like it in all the years I've spent in aviation — and that's most of my life," Macauley said. He reported to a House of Representatives subcommittee that the saucer "can skim close to the ground, dart between trees, dip into small valleys and generally hug the Earth's surface." Reports from the U.S. Air Force were not so modest about the Avro craft's capabilities, describing it as a high speed interceptor aircraft. Whatever the vehicle was, the Canadian Defense Ministry abruptly announced in 1954 that the Avro disk project was being abandoned, because it "served no purpose."

U.S. News and World Report may have been premature in blowing the whistle on saucer craft in the story "Flying Saucers - The Real Story: U.S. Built First One in 1942," in its April 7, 1950 edition:

"Flying saucers, seen by hundreds of competent observers over most parts of U.S., are accepted as real. Evidence is that they are aircraft of a revolutionary type, a combination of helicopter and fast jet plane. They conform to well-known principles of aerodynamics. An early model of these saucers was built by U.S. engineers in 1942, achieved more than 100 successful test flights. That project then was taken over by the Navy in wartime. Much more advanced models now are being built... In more detail, the story pieced together from nonsecret testimony of responsible U.S. scientists, private observers and military officials is this:

"Early models of the flying saucer... were built by U.S. Government engineers of the National Advisory Committee for Aeronautics... The first U.S. model, designed by Charles H. Zimmerman, of NACA, was elliptical in shape, powered by two piston engines and driven by twin propellors. It had a maximum speed between 400 and 500 miles per hour. More important, it could rise almost vertically and its minimum speed for landing was only about 35 miles an hour, a great advantage in military and naval aircraft...

"What they look like... is described in well-documented accounts. Those accounts show saucers to be exactly 105 feet in diameter, circular in shape. They have what appear to be jet nozzles arranged all around the outer rim, just below the center of gravity. They are made of a metal alloy, with a dull whitish color. There are no rudders, ailerons, or other protruding surfaces. From the side the saucers appear about ten feet thick - there are no exact measurements from this angle in publicly available records. They are built in three layers, with the center layer slightly larger in diameter than the other two..."

Another verification of early hidden saucer technology was received by researcher Thomas Adams, although the author (known to Mr. Adams) chose to remain anonymous:

"I was privileged once to get in on the observance of a real, genuine, solid, tangible UFO model under construction where I was once an employee at Goodyear Aerospace Corp. (now Goodyear Atomic!) in Akron for three years back in the mid-60's. I had 'blue, secret' clearance then and the individual who showed me the UFO in a special hangar there had 'red, top secret' clearance. At that time I was not allowed to disclose what I had seen due to just the fact that I was an employee. We were under the threat of a Federal fine and imprisonment if we talked about matters secret or top secret. Of course, now, it no longer applies. Anyhow, I found out later, through Mrs. C [name on file with Mr. Adams] that a [UFO investigator - name on file] had phoned her about OTHER former employees of G.A.C. having seen the same thing I did. [Mrs. C.] then proceeded to tell [the investigator] then asked me to come over to his place to identify pictures he had of it [taken by someone who sighted the UFO over in Indiana] upon which I did. It is commonly referred to as the 'Zip Craft' and is now known to fly in excess of 10,000 mph and is test-flown now and then throughout mainly Ohio, Indiana and Kentucky. The model I saw was still in the construction stages but looked to be of an aluminum-type material, flat surface with a dome in the middle, no visible portholes, about twenty feet in width, smooth as silk, antenna on top of dome, etc. I believe it was only about 60% completed so the description cannot be totally accurate as I did not see a complete 'Zip' with my own eyes other than in [the investigator's] photos and slides. To this day I have no idea how G.A.C. could have constructed a UFO capable of fantastic speeds, but my feeling is that some of the ideas may have come from knowledge obtained from inspection of crashed UFOs... Whatever the case may be, I do feel our government knows one helluva lot they're not telling the masses about."

A letter sent by Dexter W. Zinke to Lawrence Fawcett of Citizens Against UFO Secrecy in 1990 again confirms the existence of government disk craft. Zinke says: "I saw a show on *Inside Edition* yesterday that mentioned your organization and its efforts to expose the role of the U.S. Military in the UFO situation. I thought you might like to hear my experience with this subject when I was a Navy Officer stationed at Moffett Field, California.

"In November 1964 I went into Hangar No. 1, the old zeppelin hangar, and saw a flying saucer. It was about twenty feet in diameter and four or five feet thick. It had no vertical control surfaces such as rudders. It stood on small steel legs, about 3/4 inches in diameter, about two feet off of the ground. The legs did not appear to retract. It had a cockpit, covered by a hemispherical plexiglass cover, for only the pilot. I could see a couple of dozen gauges and various controls in the cockpit. It had an air intake, which was about five feet in diameter, located in the center of the top surface. Turbine blades were visible inside of the air intake. The cockpit was on one side of the aircraft between the edge of the air intake and the outer edge of the saucer. Under the saucer, around the entire outer edge, there were flaps about four inches high and two feet wide that could be moved independently from horizontal to vertical, inboard from these flaps. Exhaust gases had been directed by the flaps. The flaps and the exhaust ports were blackened. On the top of the saucer, around the edge, in black block capital letters about four inches high, was printed 'U.S. AIRFORCE-U.S. NAVY.'"

"I went and got a friend of mine, Lt Ken McCaw, who was the legal officer for Moffett Field, and took him to Hangar No. 1. He saw the saucer. Ken was here in Portland working for Georgia Pacific Corporation, but I have not talked to him in years. I really do not know where he is now. Attorneys are not too hard to find if you want to talk to him.

"There were armed Marine guards in the hangar all the time. It would be interesting to see how many would remember the saucer and come forward. When I saw the saucer in '64 it had been in storage since '58 so quite a few guards must have seen it.

"In early 65 I managed to get a tour of Ames Research Center, which was located at Moffett Field at that time. I was talking to two men there and asked if they knew about the saucer in Hangar No. 1. They both said they had, and that the saucer that I had seen flew from 1955 to 1958 and was subsonic. They said that supersonic saucers were being flown at that time ('65).

"I have kept quiet all these years because I have been afraid of retaliation by the Navy. Your program last night just goes to show that the Military covers up a lot of things and that is why so much money is wasted on defense. Maybe if more people who were in the Military would talk-up some of this waste can be stopped. If the Navy does retaliate against me it will be an excellent indication that they do know about flying saucers and have something to hide."

Popular tales of extraterrestrial abductions aside, we do know that the U.S., Canadian and British governments were conducting flights with saucer-shaped flying craft throughout the latter half of this century, and eye-witness reports and film of unusual aerial maneuvers over government bases suggest that these flights continue to this day. In recent years thousands of people have trekked into the Nevada desert to watch the lights of 'impossible' aircraft dancing in the sky above the U.S. military installation variously called Dreamland, S-4, and Area 51.

An article in the February 1987 issue of *Gung-Ho,* a magazine about the military, talks about "UnFunded Opportunities" (UFO) currently available:

"As for 'UnFunded Opportunities,' these are programs dealing with technology levels so advanced that one Air Force officer involved in SR-71 development said: 'We are flight testing vehicles that defy description. To compare them conceptually to the SR-71 would be like comparing Leonardo Da Vinci's parachute design to the space shuttle.'

"Other officers are similarly emphatic about the nature of these new systems: 'We have things that are so far beyond the comprehension of the average aviation authority as to be really alien to our way of thinking,' says one retired colonel."

Former NASA technician Bill Kaysing maintains that *We Never Went To The Moon* in his book of the same title. Having analyzed photos of Lunar landings and reviewed official NASA reports, Kaysing believes that the moon launch and other space ventures were staged and, while decoy rockets were launched, the moon landings were simulated on sound stages at secret installations in Nevada. The information that Kaysing has gathered, however, can be interpreted in a different manner.

Photos of the first Lunar landing show a strange discrepancy. There is no indication that the rocket blast from the Lunar module disturbed the soil to any degree. Footprints of the astronauts are shown in profusion around the module, yet there is no crater beneath it, not even an apparent disturbance of the dust caused by the lander's exhaust.

While this might be interpreted as proof, as Kaysing believes, that the lander was a stationary mock-up on a soundstage in Nevada, it could also be an indication that the module employed another means of propulsion that did not require rockets, such as the gravity or other drives mentioned in the *Gung-Ho* article.

Research into such propulsion methods has been conducted for many years, and used to be spoken of much more frequently than it is today, with scientists in the 1950s going so far as to suggest that a breakthrough in anti-gravity research was "imminent." Testimony to the House Armed Services Committee hearings on UFOs in 1966 revealed that "six agencies of the federal government are extending themselves in research to uncover the suspected secret of these objects [i.e. UFOs] — that of gravity control or anti-gravity power. Forty-six such projects of research of varying degrees are currently being subsidized, including 33 under Air Force supervision."

Were all those projects unsuccessful?

6

Hot Jobs and Crop Circles

*A*lternative 3 relates the assassination of scientist "Sir William Ballentine" by laser "hot job." Quoting Professor Hubert Radwell ...who gave evidence at the Ballentine inquest:

"Ballentine's body was not merely burned. It was reduced to little more than cinders and scorched bones. His skull had shrunk because of the intense heat to which he had been subjected and yet his clothing was hardly damaged."

A real parallel to laser hot jobs are other secret plans of the Nazis in the last days of the war.

Albert Speer, in *Inside the Third Reich* relates that in April, 1945 he was told by Robert Ley, Germany's Minister for Labor, that Germany possessed a "death ray." Heinz Schaeffer corroborated Speer in his book *U-boat 977*, saying that the S.S. had offered to give him a demonstration of a "death ray," also in April of 1945, but that due to his schedule as a submarine captain he had been unable to attend.

The U.S. government-published *America's Aircraft Year Book* provides further information on plans related to a death ray: "Rudolph Herrman... a specialist in supersonics... was a member of the group entrusted with Hitler's futuristic plans to establish a space-station rocket refuelling base revolving as a satellite about the Earth at a distance of 4,000 miles." Major Robert Staver, one of Herrman's interrogators, described plans to equip the space station with a giant focusing reflector. "[It is] a weapon which will enable the first country to achieve this undertaking to rule the world. The focusing of this reflector upon any living persons would kill them immediately. Ocean water would be instantly turned to steam, a forest instantly kindled."

During World War II the Japanese were also involved in exotic weapons research, as evidenced by a document from the library of the Imperial War Museum in London. Titled "RESTRICTED APPENDIX 1-E, SUBJECT: DEATH RAY" and dated 3 October, 1945, it is a synopsis of interviews with Lieutenant General Shimoda and other Japanese officers, conducted by Doctors Griggs, Moreland, and Stephenson. The document states:

"For five and a half years the Japs have been working on a 'death ray.' This is based on the principle that very short radio waves focused in a beam of high power will cause physiological effects in mammals, resulting in death. The purpose of these researches was to develop a military weapon which would cause paralysis or death to any human being upon whom the beam was focused." The document goes on to describe the device's most suitable military application, "anti-aircraft," and to say that the Japanese had spent the equivalent of two million dollars in its development. Also described are various experiments using the death ray, and the amount of time required to kill animals of differing species, concluding: "With the development of higher-power and shorter-wave length oscillators, which has become possible through the Allied research on radar, it is possible that a death ray might be developed that could kill unshielded human beings at a distance of five to ten miles if these Japanese experiments are reliable indications of the potentialities of the death ray."

How does this relate to current technological capability, or the revealed hints of such? Apparently America does have functional battlefield lasers as part of its weapons arsenal. The *Spotlight* newspaper described the Pentagon's secret "Project AOC" (Army Optical Countermeasures) and the usage of "A high-frequency laser gun pulsating 10 joules of beam power 100 times per second... [to] incinerate a human eye." A joule is the amount of energy need to accelerate a quarter-pound weight to 100 feet per second. In the article authors Harrer and Dobbs relate their sources had said the weapon was deployed during the Iraqi war.

Another interesting clue to possible covert research are the reports of arson investigators seeking the cause of a large number of forest fires in central California in 1985, as noted by researcher Waves Forest. Research suggests that the burn patterns of the fires were started high in the trees, with the effects of lightning being ruled out. Fantastically, these high level burns could indicate the firing of laser weapons (perhaps part of the government Star Wars program) from some point in the atmosphere or in space.

A strange, although factual case was related in the *Society for the Protection of Individual Rights and Liberties (SPIRAL)* newsletter of August 21, 1982:

"The... case discussed here... concerns Jack Angel, 66... a successful, healthy clothing salesman who happened to be on the road making a sales trip when it happened. On November 12, 1974, Jack pulled his motorhome into a Ramada Inn parking lot in Savannah, GA and prepared himself for a good night's sleep. However, Jack didn't wake up until four days later, on Nov. 16. He was severely burned.

"As Jack explained it, 'It was just burned, blistered (his hand), and I had this big explosion in my chest. It left a hell of a hole. I was burned down here on my legs and between my groin, down on my ankle and up and down my back. In spots!' But he felt no pain. He showered and changed his clothes (none of which were touched by the burn). He staggered to the lounge (although he had not been drinking) and ordered a scotch to ease the pain. Suddenly Jack got up and staggered to the restroom. The next thing he recalls is being in a hospital. He had a charred hand and a 3 x 4 centimeter burn cavity in his chest. The doctors told him he had been burned *internally*!

"Jack and his wife checked out the mobile home to see what could have caused these burns, but she found nothing unusual. During this time Jack had to have his hand amputated because of damaged nerves and burns. After recuperating he got in touch with lawyers to see if he could seek damages for a possible malfunction in his motorhome, but the lawyers checked and rechecked every detail of the motorhome — they even checked the power lines above the space where he parked those 4 nights, but no cause could be found and the case was dropped. To this day, Jack does not know how he became so severely burned."

In discussing recent "crop circle" phenomena in the *Amargi* ecology newsletter, author Otter G'Zell suggests a possible explanation involving military hardware that may be employed in "hot jobs." "A ...mundane and disturbing hypothesis has been proposed [for the crop circles] by Jean-Jacques Velasco, head of GEPAN (*Groupe d'Etudes des Phenomenes Aerospatiaux Non-identifies*), the official UFO investigative agency of the French government (now renamed SEPRA). Velasco has pointed out the large number of military installations in the area of the phenomena (although a third of Wiltshire is off-limits to the public). The military claims vast tracts of land to which it allows only severely restricted access, including no non-military overflights, and it is significant that the 'crop circles' in Britain, as well as those in the U.S., Canada and New Zealand, are showing up on these very military reservations! Velasco believes that the circles are a result of military tests of advanced Star Wars weaponry, perhaps created by a beam of infrared or microwave energy bounded off mirrors in space to the fields below.

"Velasco's hypothesis would also account for the lack of an uproar among the farmers: perhaps they are being compensated? It would also explain why none of England's professional biologists have taken the trouble to visit the sites, although Oxford, Cambridge and other prestigious universities are an easy drive away.

"In consultation with our own investigators, the ERA is tending to concur with Dr. Velasco. Several significant details have been reported to us which we think may allow a tentative reconstruction of the mechanism involved: First, we have the report of a laboratory analysis of some of the affected wheat stalks. The 90 degree bending at the base is due to the 'explosion' of the lowest node of the stalk, evidently by vaporization of the water contained therein. Deprived of its structural rigidity at the node, the stalk simply falls over. The fibers are not broken in the process, and continue carrying water and nutrients past the collapsed node, so the plant continues living where it has fallen. This effect can most readily be explained by microwaves, which can be tuned to a frequency that will vaporize water. Indeed, microwave lasers, called 'masers' (Microwave Amplification by Stimulated Emission of Radiation), were actually developed some years before the now-familiar visible-light lasers.

"The second relevant report comes from a farmer who claims to have witnessed the formation of a circle. He says that it was as if a giant hand suddenly laid down on the wheat with a rapid rotation, twisting it into a flattened spiral. The image of a collapsing spiral of dominos leaps to mind. This effect would be expected of a rotating maser beam directed from above.

"But the most telling report, and one which offers the most concrete evidence we have so far come across, comes from a recreational glider pilot who drifted with the air currents over restricted military airspace in Wiltshire. He observed a reflection of his glider floating in the air before him, and as he sailed closer he found himself circling a huge but invisible cylindrical reflecting surface suspended vertically in the air.

"I offer this hypothetical reconstruction of a top-secret military device capable not only of creating the mysterious 'crop circles,' but also of being a devastating anti-personnel weapon. Imagine a huge vertical cylinder made of rigid 100% reflective mylar. The top is capped with a slightly bulging disk of flexible reflective mylar, similar to that found in popular helium balloons. The bottom is capped with a transparent mylar disk. Inside, the upper disk is sealed to a clear underdisk. By injecting or removing air into the space between, the parabolic shape of the upper mirror may be increased or decreased to focus a beam reflected off its surface. In the center of the cylinder is a rotating maser projection device. This is aimed upward at the curved top mirror, so the entire apparatus resembles a giant upside-down reflecting telescope.

"A maser altimeter and computer-adjusted air pressure devices adjust the focus of the reflected beam to any configuration desired at ground level. Atmospheric buoyancy is achieved by filling the entire cylinder with hydrogen. Position would be controlled by gas jets. It obviously wouldn't be stable in a high wind, but in still air the device could be maneuvered into position, fired and returned to base with no one the wiser. The exterior surface would reflect only sky and be completely invisible to the eye unless one were directly under it and looking up into the interior, where relatively small mechanisms might be seen. Even these could be cloaked by suspending a reflective cone directly beneath the interior mechanisms. As for the more complex patterns in the affected wheat fields, these could be achieved in the same manner as Batman's 'bat-signal,' by superimposing a cut-out template between the maser beam and the upper parabolic mirror."

If crop circles are the result of military or other advanced weapons testing, they may have two purposes. The initial crop circles were just that, simple round impressions with, at times, outriggers of smaller circles. With time and numerous appearances of the "circles," however, the manifestations have gotten more complex, modified into vast configurations of arcs, triangles, circles and lines, resembling the arcane sigils of any number of occult groups — and certainly not random "whirlwind" or magnetic vortex events. Some investigators have gone so far as to suggest that there are messages in the crop formations, and some claim to have deciphered them.

If the crop circles are being inscribed by the use of laser or microwaves on rural landscapes from the upper atmosphere or outer space, possibly to test focal length and the aim of these advanced weapons, then making them represent mystical patterns might serve a purpose. It would channel public attention into arcane realms (such as UFOs from outer space), and make the circles appear to be extraterrestrial messages — not military test patterns.

7

Missing Scientists and LGIBs

*I*n the book *Alternative 3*, Watkins and Ambrose develop page-long biographies of three "missing scientists" to flesh out their brief treatment in the television show: Ann Clark, Brian Pendlebury, and Robert Patterson.

"Ann Clark" is presented in a mini-soap opera revealing no details of her professional, scholastic, or community life, but instead going into detail about her being dumped by her fiancee "Malcolm" and the frustration she felt — the upshot being that this makes her want to relocate to Mars.

Another scientist, "Brian Pendlebury," is reported to have left an undisclosed university with a degree in electronics to take a job with "a major electronics firm in Sydney, Australia." For five months he stays in touch with his parents, who have a "cozy vision of Brian marrying some nice sensible Lancashire girl and of [his mother] becoming a doting grandmother." But when they try to locate him in Australia he does not live at the address listed on his letters, and the company he is supposedly working for has never heard of him. Or so they say, nudge, nudge.

"Robert Patterson" a "senior lecturer... at the University of St. Andrews" and "one of the most brilliant mathematicians in Britain" is unhappy about high English taxation and announces that he is going to America. He abruptly vanishes. There is no word whether an LGIB (Lancashire-girl-in-black) is also involved in this disappearance.

These profiles, presented in classic *True Confessions* style, do not do credit to a serious theme. There was a British "brain drain" in the 1970's, consisting of large numbers of British scientists leaving the country for employment in other countries, and there have been missing and murdered scientists.

Other missing scientists mentioned in *Alternative 3* include:

Richard Tuffley, Swansea, South Wales, January 5, 1976; Gordon Balcombe, Bromley Kent, February 5, 1976; Sidney Dilworth, Reading, Berkshire, April 16, 1976; Andrew Nisbett, Houston, Texas, October 5, 1976; Pavel Germanas, Jerusalem, Israel, July 14, 1977; Marcel Rouffanche, Paris, France, November 16, 1977; and Eric Hillier, Melbourne, Australia, December 29, 1977.

So far as I can determine, these individuals and their disappearances were all invented for *Alternative 3*. There was, however, what seems to be a concerted effort by unknown individuals to sabotage SDI research by murdering scientists during the same period of time when the Soviets were attempting to achieve the same result by negotiation. This may have been part of an assassination program in existence at the time of the airing of *Alternative 3* on television, although the press only takes note of deaths beginning in 1982 — an example of strange prescience in *Alternative 3*.

A partial list of SDI-connected scientists who committed suicide or died under mysterious circumstances (none, so far as can be determined, by "hot job") includes:

In March of 1982, Keith Bowden, an expert on supercomputers and computer-controlled aircraft; killed when his car went off an embankment.

March of 1985, Roger Hill, a designer at Marconi Defense Systems, allegedly committed suicide by shotgun blast.

In November of 1985, Jonathan Walsh, a digital communications expert employed by Marconi's parent firm, GEC, fell from his hotel room. He had expressed fear for his life.

On July 9, 1986, Karl-Heinz Beckurts and his driver were killed by a bomb near Munich. Beckurts was Director of Research at Siemens Company, an SDI contractor allegedly linked to activities of Otto Skorzeny's Nazi International.

August 1986: Vimal Dajibhai, employed in computer-guidance with Marconi, jumped from a bridge in Bristol England.

On October 10, 1986, Gerrold von Braunmuhl was assassinated outside Bonn, West Germany. Von Braunmuhl had been a chief advisor to West German Foreign Minister Hans-Dietrich Genscher during SDI talks.

In October of 1986, Ashad Sharif, another employee of Marconi, apparently tied a rope to his neck, got in his car, and drove off, with fatal results.

On July 30, 1986, Swedish professor Svante Oden disappeared.

Also in 1986, Lando Conti, the head of an electronics company and associate of the Italian defense minister, was killed in an unspecified fashion.

There were at least four deaths or disappearances of scientists in January of 1987. These included:

Aytar Singh-Gida, working on SDI-related technology, who disappeared.

Richard Pugh, who had worked on Defense Ministry contracts, was found dead. The circumstances were not explained.

John Brittan, a computer expert at the Royal Armaments Research and Development Establishment was found dead in his garage of apparently self-inflicted carbon monoxide poisoning.

The Swedish arms inspector Carl Fredrik Algernon supposedly committed suicide.

On February 21, 1987, Peter Peapell, a lecturer at Britain's Royal Military College, died of allegedly self-inflicted carbon monoxide poisoning in his garage.

In February of 1987 Victor Moore, design engineer with Marconi, was found dead of a drug overdose.

Also in February of 1987, Edwin Skeels, an engineer at Marconi, was found dead of carbon monoxide poisoning.

On March 20, 1987, General Licio Giorgieri was shot in Rome. Giorgieri was the Director General of Space and Armaments Procurement for the Italian Defense Ministry. March 30, 1987: David Sands, a computer expert with Easams, an SDI contractor, was killed when his car crashed. The trunk of the car was loaded with containers of gasoline.

In April of 1987, Mark Wisner, a computer specialist with the Royal Air Force weapons-testing base, allegedly committed suicide with a plastic bag over his head.

In April of 1987, Stuart Gooding, a research student at the Royal Military College of Science died in a "mysterious" car wreck.

Also in April of 1987, George Kountis, systems analyst at British Polytechnic, drowned after his car plunged into the Mersey River in Liverpool.

In May of 1987, Richard Greenhalgh, a computer salesman with the Defense Center of ICL, a principal contractor for the Royal Navy, is alleged to have slashed his wrists and leaped off a bridge.

Also in May of 1987, Michael Baker, who had worked in SDI-related areas, died in a car crash.

In June of 1987 Frank Jennings, an electronic weapons engineer, died of a heart attack. No inquest was held.

In February of 1988, Russell Smith, a scientist for the ultra-secret United Kingdom Atomic Energy Authority, allegedly committed suicide, but the authorities have neglected saying how.

In March of 1988, Trevor Knight, another employee of Marconi, died of carbon monoxide poisoning in his car.

July 19, 1989: George Koopman, a technologist at the American Rocket Company was killed in an auto accident.

In August of 1988: Peter Ferry, marketing director for Marconi, was found dead with electric leads in his mouth.

Also in August of 1988, Alistair Beckham, an engineer with Plessey Defence Systems, was found dead with electric leads to his body and a handkerchief stuffed in his mouth.

In September of 1988, Andrew Hall was found dead in his car of carbon monoxide poisoning, a hose connected to the exhaust.

Lieutenant Colonel Anthony Godley, employed at the Royal Military College of Science, disappeared in 1988.

During this period there were also bombings of companies engaged in SDI research, including Fraunhofer Research, the Dornier Company, the IBM Research Center, and the Research Institute of Optics (all located in West Germany), CSF Thomson in Paris, France, and the AEG Company in Copenhagan, Denmark.

In July of 1986, Kurt Rebmann, Germany's Federal Prosecutor, told the New York Times that he believed the attacks were part of "a coordinated offensive" against the West and SDI.

So who killed the Star Wars scientists? In at least two of the cases, those of Beckurts and von Braunmuhl, the Marxist Red Army Faction (RAF) claimed responsibility. In Italy a note was found at the location of Giorgieri's murder, stating he "was struck down exclusively for his responsibility exercised following the Italian adhesion to the Star Wars project" and attributing the murder to the Italian Red Brigades. Of course notes can be easily faked, and the fact that responsibility was claimed in only three cases is odd if two groups performed all of the murders.

A suggestive link in the chain is the minimum of five scientists who apparently died of carbon monoxide poisoning. As part of its M-K-Search operations in the 1960s, CIA-funded researchers concocted a chemical meant to simulate death by carbon monoxide poisoning. Still, if the CIA was involved, why would they want to kill the scientists?

One possibility is that it was apparent to the Kremlin that SDI, far from being the defensive program that it was presented as by Ronald Reagan, had an offensive capability. Once in place, the Russians may have reasoned, the Cold War race for military supremacy would be over. Using advanced radar imaging capability able to target individuals and missile launch facilities (which might, as the American military has suggested, include the ability to "see" through walls), the West would have a first-and-final strike ability enabling a war to be fought and won. This would make it imperative that everything possible be done to stop SDI research.

It has also occurred to me that if there is a secret disk technology on this planet, withheld for its surprise strike capability from some unknown quarter, then SDI might have been seen as a technology capable of pinpointing and shooting down such craft.

Other information touching upon the missing scientist theme in *Alternative 3* is the story related to me by author David Hatcher Childress. Speaking with a University of Colorado professor, Childress had said that he was very doubtful about the book's validity. The professor, however, wasn't so certain. He confided that he personally knew a scientist who had been offered a secret assignment dealing with computer/biological interfacing, and that the scientist had been told he would be going somewhere that "he would never return from." Promised the opportunity to "do great science," and to have all of his needs, both personal and scientific, provided for in a lavish manner for the rest of his life, he agreed. The contract the scientist signed stipulated that he was allowed to bring one other person along to the unspecified project location and, since he was unmarried, he brought his mother. He left on the specified date, and was said to have gone first to Guantanamo Bay in Cuba, from there to his final destination. When the professor later attempted to contact him through one of his colleagues, he was reminded that the man would never be returning, and was told that there were dangers involved in pressing his inquiry any further.

Pure *Alternative 3*, one might say, but Childress believes that the man was telling the truth.

Another possible confirmation of elements in *Alternative 3* is provided in a letter received by the editors of *World Watchers International* magazine from a "Mr. MJ" in El Paso, Texas:

"Back during 1978 or thereabouts, I happened on a copy of the paperback book *Alternative 3*, which detailed some of the things my father had told me years earlier, that the military had disc-shaped aircraft. A short time later, on a business trip, I met a woman and tried to impress her by mentioning that I worked as a Congressional liason to the Pentagon for Nixon's Congressman during the Watergate fiasco, and that my wife had worked as a secretary to Donald Segretti, head of CREEP, in the Naval Annex. She told me she too had worked at the Pentagon, behind the 'Green Door,' as a cryptoanalyst for military intelligence, and personal secretary to an Admiral in the late '50s.

"She was offered an assignment in Pasadena in 1962, at the Jet Propulsion Labs there, and assigned to a classified section as a photo interpreter. She scanned all in-coming photographs of the moon and Mars with 'high resolution' photography. Her husband, who she met there, worked in another department as a designer. His function was to design domed, modular living facilities for 'colonies' on the moon and then Mars! The secret name of this amazing project was 'Adam and Eve.' Her husband designed these domed structures, and all the life-support systems inside and out. One of their local probes had found gale-velocity winds on Mars, and no other structure would hold up.

"Sometime later, her husband and several other key scientists were chosen for an even more secret project, and went off to parts unknown. She never saw him again. When she asked, she was told that his whereabouts were on a need-to-know basis. She got letters from him, but no hint of where he was. One day she was told that he had been killed, but no further information and no body were provided. Then her 'Q' clearance was pulled. When I asked her jokingly if she thought her husband had been drafted to go to Vietnam, she stared at me and replied, 'No, I think he was drafted to Mars!' And she was dead serious."

8

Ice Picks, Electrodes and LSD

*I*f, as *Alternative 3* maintains, mass enslavement is the plan (if not part of the public expression) of the secret rulers and shakers of this planet, then means for making the populace controllable as a step towards complete enslavement might be desirable. Although subjugation of his neighbor has been a pet project of humanity since the beginning of recorded history, since the middle of this century the technology for creating zombies has been turned by "scientists" into a fine, if horrifying, art.

Lobotomies began to be used as a technique of social control in the late 1940s. Finally the keepers could interiorize the cumbersome strait jacket. Scheflin and Opton in *The Mind Manipulators* state that 100,000 people received lobotomies between 1946-1955, with half of the operations occurring in the U.S.

Patricia Derian, during the 1940s a student nurse at the University of Virginia in Charlottesville, described a typical lobotomy, performed in an amphitheater with witnessing doctors:

"As each patient was brought in, Dr. Freeman would shout at him that he was going to do something that would make him feel a lot better. The patients had been given electroshock just before they were brought in; that's probably why he yelled at them. The shock was the only medication they received, he gave nothing for the pain, no anesthesia, no muscle relaxant.

"After the patient was placed on the table, Dr. Freeman would clap his hands and his two assistants would hold up an enormous piece of green felt the color of a pool table. That was the photographic backdrop. Dr. Freeman would direct the placement of lights so that each operation could be photographed, and he checked carefully to be sure that the cameraman was ready, that they had a good angle showing Dr. Freeman with his instrument, that there was no shadow to spoil the picture. His main interest during the entire series of lobotomies seemed to be on getting good photographic angles. He had each operation photographed with the icepick in place.

"When all was ready, he would plunge it in. I suppose that was part of his surgical technique, if there is a technique for such surgery. You probably have to plunge it in to break through the back of the eye socket. He lifted up the eyelid and slid the icepick-like instrument over the eyeball. Then he would stab it in suddenly, check to be sure the pictures were being made, and move the pick from side to side to cut the brain."

By at least the 1940s American clandestine organizations were engaged in on-going secret programs of lobotomy, chemo-psychiatric and other mind manipulation that continues unabated and fine-tuned to this day.

George Estabrooks of Colgate University proposed the use of hypnosis during warfare to the Department of War prior to World War II. Since he burned the diaries relating his activities during these years, we can only speculate as to how his researches were put into practice. During the same period, Nazi psychiatrists were testing the drug mescaline on concentration camp inmates, and the OSS conducted research into behavior modification through experimentation with mescaline, barbituates, peyote, and other drugs.

In 1947 the U.S. Navy instituted Project Chatter (later renamed Project Castigate) at the University of Rochester, continuing their drug experimentation, and the CIA launched Project Bluebird, authorized by Director Roscoe Hillenkoetter (of the probably bogus MJ-12 document fame), both projects run with virtually unlimited "black budget" funding. In 1952 Project Bluebird was renamed Operation Artichoke, reportedly because Allen Dulles was fond of the vegetable.

Television, arguably a form of semi-lobotomization, was introduced to the American public in the late 1940s, providing instant access to the public mind — and access to the media sorcerers and their bosses — the Rockefellers, notably, with controlling shares in all the major networks — have.

In addition to an undeniable agenda of consumerism and prepared politics broadcast by television, there have also been a number of verified applications of subliminal programming that have taken place. These include a patriotic Statue of Liberty emblem inserted into a Saturday morning ALF cartoon, Francois Mitterand re-election slogans injected into television programming in France, and, according to an underground document circulated among anarchists in New Zealand, the "Kiwi Gemstone," CIA-sponsored Australian television subliminals.

The "Kiwi Gemstone" states that CIA subliminals were aired beginning in 1984, with the following chronology:

"24th May 1984: Four-man CIA team co-ordinated by Ray Cline arrive in Aotearoa [New Zealand] to begin installing equipment for subliminal television advertising at five sites - Waiatarua, Mt. Erin, Kaukau, Sugarloaf, and Obelisk. Sophisticated equipment can be installed within one kilometer of TV relay aerials and all linked to one IDAPS computer bureau in Auckland. Same equipment installed in Australia in August 1985; Japan in September 1986; U.K. in February 1987; New York in 1987.

"17th July 1984: In Aotearoa, subliminal advertising begins on Channel Two between 6 p.m. and midnight - hours later extended to begin at noon. Subliminal messages prepared in the U.S. by the CIA, and with the Kiwi election imminent, tell voters to support the Labour Party, the New Zealand Party, and to buy Mafia company products.

27th February 1987: New subliminal messages appear on Kiwi TV screens - "Hello, Friends. Make More Money. Vote Labour." Other messages include: "Greetings My Own. Buy Cars. Buy Now," and the most sinister of all, "Smash. Hate. Rape. Punch. Kill. Use Violence." These messages were reportedly broadcast on Australian television an average of four times per hour during this period.

A number of sources claim that during the Korean war the American use of germ warfare was concealed by maintaining that prisoners, who had been shown unopened canisters of these agents by their Korean captors, had been "brainwashed." Three journalists who claimed these chemical agents were used were arrested and put in jail in the United States.

Regardless of the truth of the claims of Korean brainwashing, these reports provided the rationale for instituting a stepped-up program of CIA mind control research dubbed M-K-Ultra, absorbing Project M-K-Delta, which had researched chemical and biological warfare. M-K-Ultra included such varied behavior control approaches as psychoactive drugs (including LSD, beginning in 1952), hypnosis, bio-electrics, radio brain bombardment, brain surgery, electronic destruction of memory, occult and parapsychological research, radiation, microwaves, and ultrasonics. "Expendables," i.e. persons whose lives could be terminated without concern of investigation, were used in these tests. M-K-Ultra existed outside of usual CIA channels, without "the usual contractual arrangements," and was "highly compartmented." The program included the participation of Nazi scientists recently imported through Project Paperclip.

CIA director Allen Dulles, speaking of personnel to be employed in administering mind control experiments, said in 1952: "Each person's ethics must be such that he would be completely cooperative in any phase of our program regardless of how revolutionary it may be." Dulles was echoing the dominant psychiatric and medical "think" of our era, as exemplified, for instance, by Edward O. Wilson in *Sociobiology: The New Synthesis:* "Scientists and humanists should consider together the possibility that the time has come for ethics to be removed temporarily from the hands of the philosophers and biologicized..."

As an indication of how far mind control research had gone, in 1953 John C. Lilly (later famous for his dolphin research and alleged ET contacts) was asked to brief members of the clandestine community on his work involving brain stimulation using electrode brain implants (a technique which had been experimented with as far back as 1898, by J.R. Ewald, professor of physicology at Straussbourg). Lilly refused, but commented: "Dr. Antoine Remond, using our techniques in Paris, has demonstrated that this method of stimulation of the brain can be applied to the human without the help of the neurosurgeon; he is doing it in his office in Paris without neurosurgical supervision. This means that anybody with the proper apparatus can carry this out on a person covertly, with no external signs that electrodes have been used on that person. I feel that if this technique got into the hands of a secret agency, they would have total control over a human being and be able to change his beliefs extremely quickly, leaving little evidence of what had been done."

Some of the medical facilities alleged to have been involved in CIA mind control work are the Mayo Clinic, Detroit Psychopathic Clinic, the National Institute of Health, Mount Sinai, the University of Michigan Medical School, the University of Minnesota Medical School, Boston Psychopathic Hospital, Allen Memorial Institute at McGill University in Montreal, Cornell University Medical School, Valley Forge General Hospital, Columbia University, the University of Oklahoma, the Addiction Research Center at Lexington, Kentucky, the University of Chicago, the University of Rochester, and the University of Illinois Medical School. And this list is far from complete.

Individuals such as Velma Orlikow would seek treatment for depression (in this case from Dr. Ewen Cameron, who was financed by the CIA and later to be President of the American Psychiatric Association, the Canadian Psychiatric Association, and the World Association of Psychiatrists) and instead would receive large doses of desonyn and sodium amytal, months of what Cameron dubbed "psychic driving" (repetition of a command tape loop for 16-24 hours a day in order to break down "psychological barriers"), electroshock, and 16 LSD trips.

Jean Charles Page, seeking treatment for alcoholism, was subjected to LSD and electroshock "depatterning" by Cameron, and placed in "continuous sleep" for 36 days, in the process becoming addicted to barbiturates.

Robert Logie, desiring treatment for leg pains, was "depatterned" with drugs and electroshock treatments, given multiple LSD trips, and placed in drug-induced sleep for 23 days.

These experimental "treatments" were performed in a variety of settings at Cameron's facility in Toronto, including the "Zombie Room," where twenty patients were kept in drugged comas for weeks at a time, the "Grid Room," where experiments in remote telemetry were performed on patients in electrode-monitored restraint, and the "Isolation Chamber," essentially a padded cell where patients could be kept for periods of time up to years in order to remove them from "outside influences."

These are a few examples of a nightmare that was replayed many thousands of times on both soldiers and civilians during the period from 1950 until the present. In the case of Dr. Cameron, who also employed lobotomy in his practice, it was later shown that his test subjects were primarily immigrants from Eastern Europe. Gordon Thomas in *Journey into Madness* has said of Cameron that, "Clearly, he saw that his tests could be extended to immigration screening."

When concerns were voiced by patients' families that these psychiatric guinea pigs were being reduced to a state of total amnesia, Cameron simply reported that the families would have to "help them build a scaffold of normal events."

In 1963 CIA Deputy Director for Plans Richard Helms related in a memo to the Deputy Director of the CIA: "For over a decade the Clandestine Services has had the mission of maintaining a capability for influencing human behavior... if we are to continue to maintain a capability for influencing human behavior, we are virtually obliged to test on unwitting humans."

Author Martin Cannon has reported that "According to declassified documents in the [John] Marks files, a major difficulty faced by the M-K-Ultra researchers concerned the 'disposal problem.' What to do with the victims of CIA-sponsored electroshock, hypnosis and drug experimentation? The company resorted to distressing, but characteristic, tactics: They disposed of their human guinea pigs by incarcerating them in insane asylums, by performing icepick lobotomies, and by ordering 'executive actions.'"

It seems never to have occurred to anyone that the madmen were running the asylums (not to mention the country), and it also seems to have eluded attention that prosecutions should take place to partially rectify the thousands of criminal acts that continue to be committed under the guise of "scientific research."

In the 1960s Dr. Louis Jolyon "Jolly" West, director of the Neuropsychiatric Institute at UCLA, proposed the utilization of an abandoned Nike missile base in California for the creation of the Center for the Study and Reduction of Violence. West was also the psychiatrist imported from the West Coast to Dallas to analyze the imprisoned Jack Ruby, assassin of Lee Harvey Oswald.

In a letter to Dr. J.M. Stubblebine, Director of Health in the California Office of Health Planning, West said of the violence reduction center that "Comparative studies could be carried out there, in an isolated but convenient location, of experimental or model programs for the alteration of undesirable behavior." West stated that the factors indicating a predisposition to violence were "sex (male), age (youthful), ethnicity (black) and urbanicity" and elaborated on his plans in a secret memo: "...Now by implanting tiny electrodes deep within the brain [it] is even possible to record bioelectrical changes in the brain of freely moving subjects, through the use of remote monitoring techniques. They are not yet feasible for large scale screening that might permit detection of a violent episode. A major task of the center should be to devise such a test..."

Included in these plans were central monitoring stations which would track individuals deemed potentially dangerous by the psychiatrists, and enable intervention with psychotropic drugs at the first spiked graph.

California Governor Ronald Reagan agreed with West that such a "violence reduction center" was a terrific idea and lobbied President Nixon, the Secretary of Defense and various federal agents, making the center a theme in his 1974 State of the State message. Stunned at statements of the California legislature that the subject was a "sensitive" matter with the public, Reagan retained the violence center in his active file until elected President.

In 1970 psychologist James V. McConnell was able to state in *Psychology Today*:

"The day has come when we can combine sensory deprivation with drugs, hypnosis and astute manipulation of reward and punishment to gain almost absolute control over an individual's behavior. It should be possible then to achieve a very rapid and highly effective type of positive brainwashing that would allow us to make dramatic changes in a person's behavior and personality... We should reshape society so that we all would be trained from birth to want to do what society wants us to do. We have the techniques now to do it.

"...We'd send him [the criminal] to a rehabilitation center where he would undergo positive brainwashing... We'd probably have to restructure his entire personality... No one owns his personality... You had no say about what kind of personality you acquired, and there's no reason to believe you should have the right to refuse to acquire a new personality if your old one is anti-social." Or, McConnell ommitted saying, if it doesn't happen to agree with the mindset of the ruling regime.

In the early 1970s Joseph A. Meyer, of the National Security Agency (obtaining, at that time, twice the funding of the CIA), proposed intercerebral implantation for approximately half of all individuals arrested (not convicted) of all crimes in the United States, and the monitoring of tens of millions of American citizens. Meyer used Harlem as a theoretical model for the implementation of his proposed control system.

In 1966 the CIA's Operation Spellbinder, under the direction of Dr. Sydney Gottlieb, conducted research in order to achieve a "sleeper killer," an unknowing control subject who could be turned into an assassin upon receiving a previously implanted code word.

A possible example of this kind of programming was the case of Luis Castillo, a mind-controlled assassin captured during the 70s by the Phillipine National Bureau of Investigation. Castillo was determined to have four different personalities which had been hypnotically installed, including Sgt. Manuel Angel Ramirez of the Strategic Air Tactical Command in South Vietnam (who claimed to be an illegitimate son of Allen Dulles; not altogether impossible, since Dulles was known for his womanizing), while another personality claimed to be one of the assassins of John F. Kennedy.

Another case was that of Candy Jones, the subject of Bains' *The Control of Candy Jones*. Jones was a star-level model during the 1940s who later started a successful modelling agency. She was contacted by the CIA and induced for "patriotic reasons" to use her agency as a mail drop. Eventually she met with and was hypnotized by CIA psychiatrists (including, Jones said, Dr. William Kroger, who later worked with Louis Jolyon West at UCLA) at a Northern California facility. Jones was subjected to the whole range of CIA mind control techniques, including hypnosis, drugs, and electronic conditioning. During the course of the conditioning she had a duplicate personality installed, was made to forget the programming sessions, had the extra personality of a racial bigot overlaid on her own reportedly tolerant personality, and was programmed to commit suicide after dismissal from the agency. Something apparently went awry in the programming, however. She married radio personality "Long John" Nebel and, with the assistance of hypnotic regression, the truth about her CIA ordeal was uncovered.

Author Martin Cannon points out a possible sub-theme in the case of Candy Jones. Nebel, as a prominent radio personality, had contacts to many personalities in the UFO research community of the day. Could Jones' marriage to him have been part of a program to infiltrate or gain information on that group?

The massive influx of LSD (deemed a "NEW AGENT FOR UNCONVENTIONAL WARFARE" in a DIA memorandum of 1 August 54) into America during the 1960s may not have been an accident. Sandoz Pharmaceuticals, at the time of the discovery of LSD, was a subsidiary of I.G. Farben, and from I.G. linked to legal counsel Allen Dulles. During the '50s and '60s Dulles, as director of the CIA, ordered in excess of one hundred million doses of LSD from Sandoz for mind control projects.

Captain Al Hubbard tells a curious story. He maintains that LSD was discovered years prior to the acknowledged date, concocted as part of a project of Rudolph Steiner's Anthroposophical Society (prior to founding this group, Steiner had been the head of the German section of Blavatsky's Isis-cult Theosophy) to create a "peace pill" to spiritually transform mankind. Regarding the truth of this, I can't say; there is strong evidence, however, that the LSD "conquest" of the world was launched by followers of philosophies derived from similar British Freemasonic channels.

Secret planning sessions were reportedly held in 1952 and 1953 by Dulles, Ford Foundation director Robert Hutchins, and Dr. Humphrey Osmond, personal physician to Aldous Huxley, for Ford-funded mescaline and LSD research.

Huxley has an interesting background. He was the grandson of Thomas Huxley, one of the founders of the Rhodes Round Table group, and Aldous was educated by members of the same elite in the Dionysian "Children of the Sun" group, probably named in honor of the Illuminist Osiris-Isis orientation. Huxley was tutored at Oxford by H.G. Wells, who was in charge of British foreign intelligence during World War I, and the author of *The Open Conspiracy: Blue Prints for a World Revolution.* Aleister Crowley, "the Beast 666" and founder of the Isis-Urania Temple of Hermetic Students of the Golden Dawn, provided Huxley's initiation into psychedelic substances. It was Huxley's psychedelic/occult groups which in turn provided the launching pad for the entire roster of 60s acid gurus, including Timothy Leary, Alan Watts, Gregory Bateson, Richard Alpert and, through Bateson, Ken Kesey (of *Merry Pranksters* fame).

In England, the Tavistock Institute, connected to the psychological warfare division of British intelligence, sponsored conferences on such subjects as the "Dialectics of Liberation" hosted by Tavistock staff psychoanalyst R.D. Laing, and attended by Angela Davis and Stokely Carmichael, among others. The Tavistock Institute was funded by the Ford Foundation, the British Defense Ministry, and Harvard University.

As repugnant as it may be for a liberal audience to consider, the '60s "counter-culture" of LSD may have constituted an action reminiscent of the goals of the earlier British "vitality sapping" assault on China through opium; it may have also provided an Illuminist-derived injection of mysticism into American culture, a "peace pill."

There is a fine line to be drawn. While mysticism perhaps comprises a vital, higher form of perception, in the matter of the real world that perception needs to be checked with critical analysis. A lack of a practical understanding is one reason that the hippie revolution failed, and this perhaps inherent shortcoming of drugged enlightenment may provide a rationale for the injection of drugs and mystical philosophy into a society. It may, in fact, be a technique for "softening up" populations. Hasn't religion and mysticism always been used in this manner?

Timothy Leary is an interesting case of a hippie who possibly wasn't. Leary first obtained LSD from his longtime CIA buddy Frank Barron, a man who was at one time tapped, as Leary mentions, to become "director of psychological personnel at the CIA." In his biography, Leary seems less than forthcoming about the large number of his friends who are CIA, OSS, and members of the CFR/Eastern Establishment. These include Harry Murray (OSS chief psychologist), Robert Gordon Wasson (Vice President of J.P. Morgan & Co.), Martin Orne ("...a brilliant CIA-funded consciousness researcher... sometimes to be seen in our kitchen drinking coffee and asking intelligent questions about the relationship of drug states to hypnosis") and socialite Mary Pinchot Meyer, who had been married to top level CIA agent Cord Meyer, Jr., and may have been assassinated because of her knowledge of the JFK hit.

Not a beaded headband among that crowd.

Leary speaks in candid-yet-veiled style when he says, "By this time I felt like I was being initiated into a secret order of Cambridge Illuminati. Frank [Barron, of the CIA] smiled at the idea." And so is the reader supposed to smile, I imagine.

Leary's speaking engagements on college campuses in the 80s, engaging in debates with G. Gordon Liddy of Watergate fame, are horribly reminiscent of good cop-bad cop routines, the "cognitive dissonance" mind control technique factually employed by behavioral psychologists in public schools, or even the mocking Freemasonic psychodrama which Michael A. Hoffman II alludes to in his brilliant *Secret Societies and Psychological*

Warfare. It is as if college students were being shown that Leary and Liddy exemplified the entire left-right range of intellectual possibility available to them, much in the same manner that the Republicans and Democrats have long been presented as our only options in the political arena. And so, I suppose, it seemed to us during the '60s. It is even possible that it may seem that way to Leary and Liddy.

For my part, I don't have any evidence that Leary was a witting agent of the CIA or the Tavistock Institute or the Round Table; more likely an unwitting agent, although that "Cambridge Illuminati" crack makes me wonder. Aldous Huxley's disapproval of Leary's psychedelic missionary antics (as reflected in his correspondence) seems to support the idea that Leary was a rogue vector in a trajectory that arguably began in the vicinity of Bavarian Illuminist Adam Weishaupt, yet Leary admits that Huxley encouraged him to "become a cheerleader for evolution" with the infusion of "brain-drugs, mass-produced in the laboratories" into the population. Whether Leary saw puppet masters lurking behind the moving paisley veil, he espoused mystical doctrines identical to those of Huxley and fellow travellers in the uniquely complicated Round Table-British Intelligence- and, yes, Illuminati universe.

Another example of strange currents underlying mind control operations is provided by James Shelby Downard in his article "The Call to Chaos" in *Apocalypse Culture*, edited by Adam Parfrey. Downard says that:

"The secret society which became the nucleus of the Office of Strategic Services-Central Intelligence Agency octopus was making biotelemetry implants in unsuspecting people as early as 1933. After the operations, the victims were kept drugged for a time and then were brainwashed... I believe the implants were at first activated by touching the skin with a device similar to an electric prod...

"The early implants were made to stimulate the pudendal nerve, when triggered, so that the sexually excited and amnesiac-drugged victims could be used in the sex circuses of the OSS-CIA secret order. Those victims were not infrequently operated on while anesthetized by morphine and scopolamine, which produce analgesia and amnesia (twilight sleep, to esotericists). They too were brainwashed after healing. This evil program, supposedly for the sake of national security, was oriented to the [Freemasonic] Cult of GAOTU [Grand Architect of the Universe]... A woman I know performed in those rites some years ago, representing such deities as Artemis (Diana or Hecate), Aphrodite Porne (Dirty Venus), Bastet, Selket, and the White Goddess described by Robert Graves in his famous book. I do believe that these sex circuses were part of a greater Call to Chaos working..." Herein is a confirmation of the existence of a Freemasonic Mother Goddess cult within intelligence circles.

If the preceding theory seems fanciful, one has only to look to the ritual nature of the Jack the Ripper murders, performed by high ranking Freemasons in the British government and described by Stephen Knight in *Jack the Ripper: The Final Solution,* to the Freemasonic ritual murder of the P2's Licio Gelli, or to the Crowleyan ritual magic(k) worked in the '40s by Jack Parsons and reputed Naval Intelligence agent L. Ron Hubbard (who was to later found the Church of Scientology, based upon initiatory grades not unlike Freemasonry, and a cosmology highly reminiscent of Theosophy). Interesting leads may be provided by Hubbard's choice of names for his precursor mental therapy, Dianetics. Although he maintained it was a derivative of the Greek *dianous,* "through thought," it is difficult to determine why he would name his eldest daughter Diana in similar commemoration. The Scientology crucifix is virtually a copy of the Crowley emblem depicted in *The Book of Thoth,* while Hubbard is reported to have maintained that he was the reincarnation of Cecil Rhodes.

In recent years Dr. Michael A. Aquino, a colonel in U.S. Army intelligence and leader of a Church of Satan offshoot named the Temple of Set, has been investigated by military and civilian authorities on claims of child molestation at San Francisco's Presidio military base. Although charges against Aquino have been dismissed, reporter Linda Goldston investigated the military intelligence unit in person and reported evidence of cultic activity having taken place there, including concrete bunkers converted to "ritual chambers" and examples of what appear to be the symbolic accompaniments to Satanic rites, including painted pentagrams, black and white candle drippings, and a large drawing of Satan (or Set) emblazoned on the wall of a building which had been locked.

Aquino, aside from his status as a Satanic high priest, is an expert on military mind control and has expounded on what he terms LBM, Lesser Black Magic used in the control of civilian populaces, the techniques of which include PSYOP (psychological operations) as well as conventional forms of terrorism. Aquino has written on his theories of mind control in an article which he submitted to the Washington Military Review, titled "From PSYOP to MindWar: The Psychology of Victory." The cover page of the article states the article originates from "HEADQUARTERS, IMPERIAL STORMTROOPER FORCE/Office of the Chief of Staff/MindWar Center/Hub Four" and it is essentially a peptalk on the usage of "psychotronic" (psychological-electronic) techniques, citing in particular the usage of air ionization ("Detonation of nuclear weapons...

will alter atmospheric ionization levels") and the broadcasting of Extremely Low Frequency (ELF) waves for the manipulation of human behavior.

And then there is the black magic research the CIA funded in the 1970s. Dubbed Operation Often, CIA agents contacted the monsignor in charge of exorcisms for the Catholic Archdiocese of New York. When he refused to cooperate with them, they next approached Sybil Leek, who provided a thumbnail estimate of the Black Magic growth industry in the U.S., reportedly consisting at the time of four hundred regularly operating covens and untold thousands of freelance spell-casters. The CIA covertly funded a course in sorcery at the University of South Carolina, and Operation Often closely monitored these classes, reportedly devoted to fertility and initiation rites as well as techniques for raising the dead.

And all on your tax dollar.

9

Electronic Wars

*1*959 is the first mention of radio-controlled electronic stimulation of the brain (ESB) in M-K-Ultra documents. Although little has been intentionally revealed about this research, Martin Cannon has indicated that an anonymous informant told him, "beginning in 1963, the CIA and military's mind control efforts strongly emphasized electronics." Dr. Jose Delgado, well known for his early experimentation with intercerebral implants, has supposedly abandoned this area and gone onto research into the effects of electromagnetic fields on the human brain.

It is reported that experimentation was done by the CIA in the 1960s on RHIC-EDOM, "Radio Hypnotic Intracerebral Control" and "Electronic Dissolution of Memory." This is the use of remote induction of hypnotic trance and post-hypnotic suggestion, with an erasure of memory after the subject performs the desired acts.

Project Pandora in the 1970s researched the biological effects of Extremely Low Frequency radio emissions (ELF), including microwave and radio waves. This experimentation was reportedly done in response to the beaming of microwaves at the U.S. embassy in Moscow by the Soviets. Dr. Milton Zarat, who searched Soviet scientific literature for a clue as to the purpose of the microwave bombardment, found that, "For non-thermal irradiations, they believe that the electromagnetic field induced by the microwave environment affects the cell membrane, and this results in an increase of excitability or an increase in the level of excitation of nerve cells."

A statistically high number of illnesses were noted among Moscow embassy employees, and U.S. ambassador Walter Stoessel developed a rare blood disease similar to leukemia, suffering from headaches and bleeding from the eyes. Stoessel reported to his staff that microwaves could cause leukemia, skin cancer, cataracts and various forms of emotional problems. Chromosomal damage was noted in a high percentage of the embassy staff, while white blood cell counts were abnormally high in one third of the staff.

The Army Medical and Information Agency document "Biological Effects of Electromagnetic Radiation — Eurasian Communist Countries," released in 1974 provides a good idea of research conducted during this period. In the document the researches are attributed to "Soviet scientists," but according to Dr. Allen Frey, the experiments reported as being performed by the Soviets were in fact his. The paper states:

"...Soviet scientists are fully aware of the biological effects of low-level microwave radiation which might have offensive weapons application. Their internal sound perception research has great potential for development into a system for disorienting or disrupting the behavior patterns of military or diplomatic personnel; it could equally be used as an interrogation tool. The Soviets have also studied the psychophysiological and metabolic changes and the alterations of brain functions resulting from exposures to mixed frequencies of electromagnetic radiation... another possibility is alteration of the permeability of the blood-brain barrier. This could allow neurotoxins in the blood to cross. As a result, an individual could develop severe neuropathological symptoms and either die or become seriously impaired neurologically. ...The potential for the development of a number of anti-personnel applications suggested by the research published in the USSR, Eastern Europe, and the West... sounds and possibly even words which appear to be originating intercranially [i.e., in the brain] can be induced by signal modulation at very low average power densities..."

In 1974, J.F. Schapitz proposed a project which was later funded for the Department of Defense: "In this investigation it will be shown that the spoken word of the hypnotist may be conveyed by modulate electromagnetic energy directly into the subconscious parts of the human brain — i.e., without employing any technical devices for receiving or transcoding the messages and without the person exposed to such influence having a chance to control the information input consciously."

In his book *Microwave Auditory Effects and Applications*, Dr. James Lin elaborates on the above technique of the direct electronic communication of words to the brain, and says, "The capability of communicating directly with humans by pulsed microwaves is obviously not limited to the field of therapeutic medicine."

Microwave transmissions have other possible applications, including the conditioning of behavioral responses. According to Anna Keeler in *Full Disclosure* magazine:

"Richard Helms wrote of such a system in the mid-1960s while he was CIA Plans Director. He spoke of 'sophisticated approaches to the coding of information for transmittal to population targets' in the 'battle for the minds of men.'.. and of 'an approach integrating biological, social and physical-mathematical research in attempts to control human behavior.' He found particularly notable, 'use of modern information theory, automata theory, and feedback concepts... for a technology of controlling behavior... using information inputs as causative agents.'"

Navy Captain Paul Tyler prepared an assessment of electromagnetic weaponry for Maxwell Air Force Base in 1986, suggesting:

"Some of these potential uses include dealing with terrorist groups, crowd control, controlling breeches of security at military installations, and anti-personnel techniques in tactical warfare. In all these cases the EM [electromagnetic] systems could be used to produce mild to severe physiological disruption or perceptual disorientation."

An instance of the probable use of ELF weapons on civilians took place in January of 1985, when women protesting nuclear weapons at the U.S. Air Force base at Greenham Common in England began experiencing strange symptoms, coincident with the changing of the security system at the base from primarily human to primarily electronic. Guards patrolling the base's perimeter were reduced in number, and antennae were installed at intervals. The women experienced an assortment of symptoms characteristic of ELF exposure, including headaches, earaches, pressure behind the eyes, bleeding from nose and gums, nausea, fatigue, hearing clicks and buzzes, and heart palpitations. Electronic testing performed by a Canadian scientist and a British electronics activist group revealed distinct areas of electromagnetic activity around the women's camps.

In 1989 *Microwave News* said that Boris Yeltsin, "...has told a reporter that the KGB has an ELF device that can stop a human heart from beating. In an interview with Radio Liberty, a U.S.-backed shortwave radio station in West Germany, Yeltsin said that KGB agents told him that they have a device which emits a powerful 7-11 Hz signal which can stop the heart. According to Yeltsin, the KGB agents said that, 'If emergency medical aid isn't close at hand, it's all over.'"

This story is interesting in light of the number of witnesses connected to the JFK assassination dying from heart attacks, as noted in my book, *The Gemstone File.*

The U.S. government is in possession of a technology similar to the one of which Yeltsin has spoken, coded Project Black Beauty. Utilizing a refrigerator-sized broadcasting unit, emotional and physical effects, including heart attack, can be induced upon living targets. This technology was apparently employed on Manuel Noriega while he was hiding in the Vatican embassy in Panama after the invasion by the U.S. The compound was ringed with large speakers and blaring "heavy metal" rock music was broadcast night and day (very likely a cover for the actual purpose of the units), reportedly to "depress" Noriega. It is also reported that the Black Beauty units were used during the Iraqi war, again under the cover of broadcasting rock music at the enemy.

A report to the U.S. House of Representatives in 1984 admitted that a large number of stores in America use ultrasonic commands broadcast to "discourage shoplifting," and a report from a medical engineer in the DOD states that microwaves and other conditioning methods have been regularly used by the Israelis against the Palestinians.

Operation Pique was an American program which included experiments bouncing electromagnetic waves off the ionosphere to disrupt the mental functions of people in Eastern Europe, particularly those employed at Soviet nuclear installations. Similar experimentation by the Soviets is recounted in an article in *Leading Edge* magazine. The article may rely on speculation, yet can be substantiated in many details. I include an excerpt in the interests of research. It is titled "Electronic Warfare Still Rages":

"On July 4, 1976, the USSR commenced the regular use of giant Tesla Magnifying Transmitters aimed against the United States. The monstrous 40 million watt signals, created by three transmitters, jammed radio waves around the world and became known to ham radio operators as the 'Russian Woodpecker.' The Soviet signal was described in the November 8, 1976 issue of *Aviation Week and Space Technology:* 'The FCC has sent several protests to the USSR over interference caused by the powerful pulsed high-frequency radio signals... the pulsed signals have a repetition rate of 10/sec (10 Hz — ELF), but the bandwidth, which is extremely wide, changes from time to time... from 30kc to more than 300kc.' The DOD publication *Soviet Military Power* describes the Soviet Tesla magnifying transmitters as being 'over the horizon radar' (which is only one of the many different functions of the Tesla transmitters). This publication does openly admit that the Soviet Tesla transmitters have created an electromagnetic disturbance and an interference grid over the United States. Unfortunately, there is a big cover-up about the effects of that electromagnetic grid.

"As of 1985, the Soviets have maintained seven transmitters. There is massive evidence that the signals are deliberately being transmitted at biologically harmful frequencies. The 1986 book *The Truth about AIDS — Evolution of an Epidemic,* written by Fettner and Check, provides documentation on the origins of AIDS and its relation to the biomedical evidence regarding ELF and the destruction of the human immune system. The immune system disease was not seen until 1978 (the Soviet ELF Woodpecker signals started in July 1976 and the actual ELF grid was expanded in the fall of 1976 and in 1977). The general feeling among scientists is that 'there had to be something new to account for the illness.' None of these individual diseases is new. Most are caused by infectious agents, long present in the human population and against which most adult Americans have developed resistance. The several diseases designated AIDS are in fact old cohabitants of the body. Fettner and Check stated, 'no known virus has ever before attacked specific cells of the immune system.'"

The information we have dealt with in the preceding two chapters is based in the main (although not entirely) upon declassified, "sanitized" accounts, information that the government considers safe for dissemination to the public. It without doubt comprises the tip of an iceberg of mind control and assassination projects and policy. Can there now be any doubt that the technology for turning humans into the zombies of *Alternative 3* now exists?

10

Batch Consignments

Other dark avenues sparking the imagination for decades, if not centuries, of those creating systems of worldwide slavery reminiscent of *Alternative 3* are those of depopulation and the concentrating of populations into slave camps. Camps whose factual existence can be documented are not located on Mars or the moon, but then, who knows what can be expected in the fullness of time?

During the early 1940s Freemasonic President Franklin Roosevelt commissioned a "master geopolitical plan" on migration ("M") and settlement to propose solutions for the predicted 30,000,000 people who would be displaced by World War II. Roosevelt considered this as much of a military as a humanitarian concern, indicating that displaced "discontented can and will cause trouble, serious trouble." 666 studies were produced for the "M" Project until the final memorandum presented to President Truman in 1945. Among the notables associated with the project were General William J. Donovan of the OSS and Knights of Malta, Nelson Rockefeller, and Sripati Chandsekhar, lifetime fellow of the British Eugenics Society.

In a 1962 book discussing the "M" Project, chairman Henry Field revealed that the study was centered around "world population increase and the future relationship to food and resources," and was also "...concerned with overpopulation on Earth, interstellar migration and the quest for living organisms on other planets." Retaining an uncanny similarity to *Alternative 3*, one possibility suggested was that "temporary quarters may eventually be established on Venus or Mars," this in a chapter titled "Interstellar Migration." The study was extensively concerned with extraterrestrial possibilities and maintained that "human population will approach infinity if it grows as it has grown in the last two millennia." While Fields plays down the extraterrestrial aspect in his book, it is obvious that it was a major focus of the study, which included the construction of two radio stations that attempted extraterrestrial communication.

Speaking of the radio experiments, Fields said: "...there were certain signals which did not come in on other wave bands. These were totally illegible as far as the Morse code was concerned. I spent many hours listening to these sounds from outer space. A British ex-Naval operator was employed to attempt to decipher these signals. Nothing intelligible resulted. Finally I recorded on a series of electrical transcription or phonograph records a selection of these mysterious radio signals.

"Now, almost forty years later, I wonder, as I did then, if those signals from outer space were attempts at radio communication between rational beings and ourselves. Certainly during the next forty years we shall know the answer." Fields coyly concludes his study of the "M" Project with the dying words of Round Tabler Cecil Rhodes: "So much to do, so little done."

The Nazis, during the 1940s, were thinking along similar, if possibly less humanitarian lines for population control and disposal. As detailed in *Gehlen: Spy of the Century* by E.H. Cookridge, the Germans had plans to turn the Soviet Union into a vast slave camp after the war.

"Byelorussia (with a population of five and a half million, including the cities of Minsk, Mogilev and Vitebsk) was to be incorporated into East Prussia and resettled by Germans; a large area of western Russia was to be annexed to the Third Reich, 'colonized' under a top layer of German settlers and administered by German officials; this area, with a total population of over fifty million, was to extend to Moscow and include the Ukraine, the Crimea, the black-earth region and part of the Caucasus, including its oil-fields. The Russians and Ukrainians within this German colony were to be treated, in accordance with Aryan racial principles, as *Untermenschen* (sub-humans); they would receive only basic education and agricultural training with a view to turning them into a nation of slaves... some forty million Soviet citizens would need to be eliminated in the proposed 'colonial' regions; this would be achieved by 'natural means,' namely famine."

German and American concentration camps during World War II have been so extensively documented as to require little comment here, except to say that one aspect of the Jewish Holocaust has been little spoken of: Allied culpability. Quoting Aarons and Loftus in *Unholy Trinity: The Vatican, the Nazis, and Soviet Intelligence:*

"In April 1943, a conference of British and American officials formally decided that nothing should be done about the Holocaust, and 'ruled out all plans for mass rescue.' The Foreign Office and the State Department were both afraid that the Third Reich would be quite willing, indeed eager, to stop the gas chambers, empty the concentration camps, and let hundreds of thousands (if not millions) of Jewish survivors emigrate to freedom in the West. As late as 1943 the British Foreign Office 'revealed in confidence' to the State Department their fear that if approaches to Germany were 'pressed too much that is exactly what might happen.'

"The bigoted reality behind the Secret Report of the Easter 1943 Bermuda Conference was that not a single Allied nation wanted to let the Jews settle in their country. The unspoken consensus was that it was better to let Hitler handle them than arrange a mass evacuation to America, Britain, or Canada. In short, the Jews were expendable to the war effort."

Allied abuse of German prisoners after the conclusion of the war has been little spoken of and is another instance that puts the lie to the lily-white image that the Allies, as victors and authors of most of the history books, were able to promote.

James Bacque, researching a book about war resistance, delved into records of the American prisoner of war camps located in Germany after World War II. While official records state that the casualty rate in American camps was under two percent, in researching original records Bacque found that there had been a deliberate cover-up. Using the statistics listed in the Army's weekly Prisoner of War and Disarmed Enemy Forces ledger, Bacque was able to determine that the annual death rate of German prisoners in American camps was 33%. Records showed that General (later President) Eisenhower had also intentionally redesignated German "prisoners of war" (protected by the Geneva Convention) to "disarmed enemy forces" (with unprotected status). The story is detailed in his book, *Other Losses,* only recently released in America.

A parallel to the genocidal themes of *Alternative 3* is the King Alfred Plan, a "contingency plan" and "final solution" for the black population of America. The Plan, comprising part of the 1967 novel *The Man Who Cried I Am* by John Williams, has for years circulated among conspiracy researchers. Jim Jones, it is said, insisted it was a factual secret document.

The King Alfred Plan begins, "In the event of widespread and continuing and coordinated racial disturbances in the United States, King Alfred, at the discretion of the President, is to be put into action immediately," with participating agencies being the National Security Council, the Department of Justice, the Central Intelligence Agency, the Department of Defense, the Federal Bureau of Investigation, and the Department of the Interior, along with National Guard units, state police, city police and county police participating.

Under the plan, the United States is divided into ten national regions and, in the case of national emergency, minorities "will be evacuated from the cities by federalized national guard units, local and state police and, if necessary, by units of the Regular Armed Forces..."

The plan concludes in a grim, science fictional manner highly reminiscent of *Alternative 3*: "'O' Committee Report: Survey shows that, during a six-year period, Production created 9,000,000 objects, or 1,5000,000 each year. Production could not dispose of the containers, which proved a bottleneck. However, that was almost 20 years ago. We suggest that vaporization techniques be employed to overcome the Production problems inherent in KING ALFRED. - Secretary of Defense."

While in all probability a fictional document, there is no doubt that John Williams was responding to and protesting the genocidal mentality of the rulers of this country and this world in a book perhaps not different in purpose than *Alternative 3*.

U.S. government document H.R. 4079 cannot be defended as fictional. Introduced in the House of Representatives in 1990, this bill may give some idea of what the Powers That Be have in store for those of us not fortunate enough to belong to such select cliques as the Round Table or Skull and Bones.

Introduced by Congressman Newt Gingrich and Senator Phil Gramm, H.R. 4079 reads:

"Guided by the principles that energized and sustained the mobilization of World War II, and in order to remove violent criminals from the streets and meet the extraordinary threat that is posed to the nation by the trafficking of illegal drugs, the Congress declares the existence of a National Drug and Crime Emergency beginning on the date of enactment of the act and ending on the date that is five years after the date of enactment of this bill."

The bill goes on for 96 pages to propose draconian repression in the name of the War on Drugs, although we must remember that they are referring here only to certain drugs such as marijuana and cocaine, whose manufacturers are not the beneficiaries of visible government subsidies such as those given to the far more lethal tobacco industry.

In complete disregard for the niceties of the U.S. Constitution and the Bill of Rights, the bill provides for the arrest of large numbers of people merely suspected of drug usage or drug dealing, and once arrested the suspected individuals would be incarcerated in one of many forced labor camps, including tent cities. All Constitutional rights would be suspended upon arrest and there would be no provisions for humane housing and treatment. Those convicted of drug usage or trafficking would receive harsh mandatory sentences, without possibility of parole, up to and including the death penalty. The assets of those convicted of dealing would be forfeited, and the people who turned them in would receive a portion of those assets as a bounty.

The bill stipulates that the usual laws regarding search warrants, illegally obtained evidence and coerced confessions would be suspended, in the name of this "War." In addition, all federal limitations on drug testing of individuals would be removed.

As well as "drug traffickers" the bill explicitly targets all "violent criminals," defining such as "Every person who is convicted in a federal court of a crime of violence against a person or a drug trafficking felony, other than simple possession." The bill describes the term "crime of violence against a person" as "a federal offense that is a felony and has as an element the use, attempted use or threatened use of physical force against the person of another."

The effect of a bill such as H.R. 4079 (and similar ones crop up frequently in Congress) would be to create a *Metropolis*-like sub-society of criminalized worker drones — *Alternative 3* sans the Martian landscape. If the government and its masters are currently addicted to sucking the lifeblood of the "masses" via income taxation and other means, think of the expanse of their greed when legally permitted to incarcerate large segments (I mean larger segments) of the populace into profitable slave labor camps.

While viewed almost universally as an example of a power-crazed religious nut leading his followers to mass suicide, there is much about Jim Jones and Jonestown that suggests this was not the entirety of the story — that the "mass suicide" at Jonestown was not the accident it has been portrayed as. John Judge's research has provided the primary source for the information about Jonestown which follows.

Tent evangelist Jim Jones migrated to Brazil in 1961, ostensibly on a mission to minister to the downtrodden. During Jones' stay, transportion and food were provided by the U.S. embassy, for unspecified reasons, and at the time Jones confided to local residents that he was working for Naval Intelligence. Dan Mitrione, a lifetime friend of Jones who worked with the CIA providing interrogation and torture techniques to Third World police forces, accompanied him at that time.

Returning to the United States after the completion of his mission in Brazil, Jones established the People's Temple in Ukiah, California, with electric fences, armed guards and guard dogs. While in Ukiah, Jones made connections with many influential people, including some who were involved in the military and clandestine agencies. During this period journalist Kathy Hunter reported seven deaths of Temple members who had tried to leave the compound; Hunter was to die later under unusual circumstances. Jones mobilized his followers to help elect Moscone as Mayor of San Francisco, and the Mayor reciprocated by appointing Jones head of the San Francisco Housing Commission — one of the darker bits of humor I've run across lately. Many of Jones' followers were hired by the San Francisco Welfare Department, where it was easy to recruit large numbers of the poor and homeless for Jones' "church."

Throughout his career, many of Jones' top associates and contributors had connections to the spy community. Richard Dwyer, CIA operative and Deputy Chief of Mission for the U.S. Embassy in Guyana, was present at Jonestown — apparently in a friendly capacity —immediately prior to the grisly end. On tapes that record the massacre, Jones can be heard shouting, "Get Dwyer out of here!" By his own admission Dwyer was observed "stripping the dead" of wallets and other effects. John Burke, who Philip Agee indicates has worked for the CIA since 1963, attempted to prevent Congressman Ryan from investigating Jonestown. In addition to obstructing Ryan in his investigation of human rights violations at Jonestown, the American embassy in Guyana routinely provided Jones with copies of all Congressional inquiries about Jonestown filed under the Freedom of Information Act.

Lawrence Layton and his family were major financial backers of Jones, furnishing him with hundreds of thousands of dollars. Layton was Chief of Chemical and Ecological Warfare Research at Dugway Proving Grounds in Utah and was later Director of Missile and Satellite Development at the Navy Propellant Division at Indian Head, Maryland. Dugway Proving Grounds, interestingly enough, has been circumstantially connected to cattle mutilations, disease biowarfare, and genetics experimentation. Layton's wife's fortune came in part from I.G. Farben, the key Nazi cartel, and the Laytons' daughter was married to George Phillip Blakey, who had extensive holdings in Solvay Drugs, a division of I.G. Blakey contributed financing to Jones and was reported to have participated in other shadowy schemes, such as moving mercenaries from Jonestown to CIA-supported UNITAS forces in Angola.

The Guyana site for Jonestown has several unusual characteristics. It is a rich location for a variety of minerals, and has been the site of much mining activity. Plans to populate the area with cheap labor go back to at least 1919. Charles Garry, a lawyer for Peoples Temple (along with Mark Lane) said that Jones and Jonestown were "literally sitting on a gold mine," and mineralogical reports confirm the statement.

It may be illuminating to recall that Jonestown was built during the time of the CIA program M-K-Ultra and that the "target populaces" of this program, including blacks, prisoners, and women, are a precise statement of the population mix at Jonestown — excluding the white male overseers.

When black members of the Temple arrived in Guyana they were bound and gagged and taken to the compound. While local inhabitants were aware of the whites living in the area and saw them in the course of their daily activities, they never saw the majority black population.

Once locked in the compound, the blacks were worked 16-18 hours per day, with rations consisting of rice, bread and on occasion, it is said, tainted meat. All of the camp overseers were white (whereas 80% of Jonestown's populace was black), and most were male. They were armed and enforced work and prevented escape. These overseers, according to researcher John Judge, were not among the dead, and no attempt has been made to locate or to prosecute them.

Although the camp doctor at Jonestown kept meticulous notes and records of drugs administered, all of his records disappeared. After the massacre enough drugs were found in the compound to have drugged 200,000 individuals for a year, this supposedly having been stockpiled as medication for a population of 1,100 persons. 11,000 doses of Thorazine were found in camp stores, as well as sodium pentathol, chloral hydrate, thalium, haliopparael and largatil, these being tranquilizers or other psychoactive drugs.

$500,000 was moved out of Jonestown shortly before the mass murder or suicide, whatever it was. Michael Prokes, who carried the money, later shot himself at a press conference, where he claimed that he was an FBI agent.

The initial news coverage issued from the scene of the tragedy said that 400 people had died in a mass suicide, and that 700 had escaped into the jungle. Later reports said that 913 had died. During the first press conference it was claimed that the reason for the discrepancy was that the Guyanese who had done the initial investigation "could not count."

The cause of the deaths reported by Dr. Mootoo, a Guyanese pathologist, was not cyanide, as the American press had reported. The victims showed none of the signs of cyanide poisoning, such as the "cyanide rictus." Mootoo found needle marks on the necks of 80-90% of the victims, and came to the conclusion that all but two of the victims had been murdered, and had not, as the press reported, committed suicide.

The Jonestown bodies were delivered to the United States after excessive delay and in states of decomposition that made autopsy impossible. All identification had been stripped from the bodies (by order of the CFR's Zbigniew Brezezinsky, the order communicated by Lt. Col. Gordon Dumner, later the Deputy Director of the CIA) and there were official complaints that military coroners were performing illegal cremations.

There are questions as to whether Jim Jones really died at Jonestown, although none of these have surfaced in the mainstream press. Identifying chest tattoos do not show up on morgue photos of Jones, and the face of the corpse is unrecognizable due to the degree of decomposition. The FBI checked the corpse's fingerprints twice in the course of their investigation, although they did not consult dental records. At the time of the massacre, Jones' finances were enormous, with estimates running from $26 million to $2 billion. He had also been known to employ doubles.

Joyce Shaw, a Temple director, described Jonestown as "some kind of horrible government experiments, or some sort of sick racial thing, a plan like that of the Germans to exterminate the blacks." Joseph Holsinger, an aide to Leo Ryan, was even more explicit: "[The] possibility is that Jonestown was a mass mind-control experiment by the CIA as part of its M-K-Ultra program."

The question is obvious: were the people of Jonestown a 'batch consignment'?

11

The Depopulation Bomb

*T*here is a solution other than cyanide to what the elite consider excess population. Why not prevent the poor — for the sake of argument, let us venture a conservative 99% of the world's population — from having children altogether, or if that isn't possible, at least vastly slow their birth rates?

"Eugenics" is a term coined in the latter part of the 19th century by Englishman Francis Galton to describe the "science" of bettering human stock and the elimination of unwanted characteristics... and individuals. Galton proposed societal intervention for the furtherance of "racial quality," maintaining that "Jews are specialized for a parasitical existence upon other nations" and that "except by sterilization I cannot yet see any way of checking the produce of the unfit who are allowed their liberty and are below the reach of moral control."

A survey of eugenics in action begins with isolated incidents such as the sterilization of mentally ill by American health officials in the late 1800s and the castration of children at the Pennsylvania Training School for Feebleminded Children in 1889. The movement quickly picked up momentum.

Formally established as a study at University College in London in 1904, the first laboratory for the study of subject was constructed by Charles B. Davenport at Cold Springs Harbor on Long Island (which, perhaps significantly, was also the location of the estates of both the Dulles brothers, as well as being the current headquarters of the Human Genome Organization for DNA mapping). The institution was funded in excess of $11 million by the Harrimans and Rockefellers.

Supported in America by the Eastern Establishment, eugenics was nurtured in the hotbeds of Round Table-influenced philosophy, at Harvard, Columbia, and Cornell. The subject was popularized in Germany by Ernst Haeckel, who linked romantic German nature mysticism and the unity of the *Volk* with clinical bio-policies later instituted by Hitler.

Haeckel believed that there was no unity among the species of mankind, since "the morphological differences between two generally recognized species — for example sheep and goats — are much less important than those... between a Hottentot and a man of the Teutonic race." In the Aryan race Haeckel saw a "symmetry of all parts, and that equal development, which we call the type of perfect human beauty." He also believed the "wooly-haired" peoples "incapable of a true inner culture or of a higher mental development... no wooly-haired nation has ever had an important history."

Haeckel felt the purpose of the nation state was to enforce selective breeding, praising the practices of the Spartans who killed all but "perfectly healthy and strong children" and thus were "continually in excellent strength and vigor."

In 1906 a group of Haeckel's academic followers formed the influential Monist League, agitating for a German government patterned along social Darwinian lines.

By 1907 in America, Indiana passed compulsory sterilization for the mentally ill and other "undesirables," while 475 males received vasectomies at the Indiana State Reformatory.

In 1912 the First International Congress of Eugenics was held in London, including among its directors Winston Churchill, Alexander Graham Bell, Charles Elliot (President emeritus of Harvard University), and David Starr Jordan (President of Stanford University).

The National Conference on Race Betterment was convened in the United States in 1914, while by 1917 fifteen American states had eugenics laws on the books, almost all of them legalizing the sterilization of habitual criminals, epileptics, the insane, and the retarded.

H.H. Laughlin, the Expert Eugenics Agent of the U.S. House of Representatives Committee on Immigration and Naturalization presented a Model Eugenical Sterilization Law in 1922. This was to provide the basis for many state eugenics laws, as well as for eugenics law in Nazi Germany.

In 1928 the American Eugenics Society sponsored a contest for essays on the causes of decline in Nordic fertility, while Dr. Robie, at the Third International Congress of Eugenics, called for the sterilization of 14,000,000 Americans with low intelligence scores.

The Nazi party in Germany passed in 1933 the "Law for the Prevention of Hereditary Diseases in Posterity," also known as the "Sterilization Law," written by Professor Ernst Rudin, one of the country's leading psychiatrists. "Hereditary Health Courts" were formed, and within three years two hundred and twenty-five thousand German "undesirables" had been sterilized.

Hitler's policies have been characterized as "a rather straightforward form of German social Darwinism." Far from being original with him, his policies were expansions upon already-extant political and scientific culture.

By 1939 German policies had evolved to include euthanasia upon asylum inmates while eugenics concepts were implemented to the fullest in Nazi concentration camps during World War II.

In 1942, U.S. psychiatrist Foster Kennedy recommended the killing of retarded children. During the three-year period between 1941-1943 over 42,000 people were sterilized in America.

After World War II the idea of "eugenics" was tainted in the public mind by its association with Nazism. The term was discarded and a facelift was performed on its parent study psychiatry, which resulted in the establishment of the World Federation of Mental Health (WFMH). Since then, this group has continued to support electroshock, lobotomization, mind control and other activities already detailed, as well as employing within its ranks many German practitioners who had been happy to further Hitlerian goals during the Second World War.

What this brief survey shows is something the popular press has chosen to ignore: that eugenics programs were not the invention of mad Nazi scientists, but that the political climate of Germany allowed a full implementation of programs part and parcel of international psychiatry and medicine. Eugenics, from its beginning, was encouraged and financed by the rich, self-styled "aristocrats" of the day.

Recent programs aimed at abortion and other methods of depopulation can be traced to essentially the same Freemasonic/Round Table/Rothschild-spawned crowd; to the studies of the Club of Rome, the Trilateral Commission, and to the CFR. These groups influenced a change in U.S. policies specifically during 1966-67, when population control was adopted by the State Department as a stated goal.

The recent world depopulation push retains the flavor of eugenics biopolicy of the first half of this century in the statements of advocates such as the Eastern Establishment's Sargent Shriver, speaking before the Congressional Select Committee on Population in 1978: "...this Committee's interest [is] in improving the quality of life and enhancing the biological product of this society; rather than just controlling or limiting births."

Jaffe and Dryfoos of the federally-funded Guttmacher Institute have stated that, "With the overall decline in fertility in the United States, concern has shifted from numbers of births to insuring that those children being born have fewer physical, social, and economic handicaps."

It is odd that little mention of "the overall decline in fertility" finds its way into the Rockefeller-subsidized literature of depopulation activists. Nor was the fact that teenage pregnancy was at its lowest ebb in forty years brought up when federally mandated family planning and sex education in schools was enacted in 1978.

Studies have shown that sex education classes increase early sexual experimentation while doing nothing to reduce adolescent pregnancy. It has also been demonstrated that when such classes are discontinued, as in Utah in 1980, the incidence of teenage pregnancy decreases. Still, officials insist sex classes should extend from "kindergarten throughout a person's entire educational career." Why? Originators and administrators of the programs candidly admit that their agenda includes depopulation and eugenics.

Lester Kirkendall, a founder of the Sex Information and Education Council, wrote in 1965 that, "sex education is... clearly tied in a socially significant way to family planning and population limitation and policy..." Dr. Jane Hodgson, at the National Abortion Federation conference in 1980, was even more forthright, calling for compulsory abortion for pregnant teenagers.

The methods of sex education programs in public schools vary, but uniformly emphasize the huge expense and drawbacks of having kids, providing summaries of methods of contraception, sterilization, and abortion. Students are often taken on tours of birth control clinics, where they meet the staff, fill out patients' forms, and are assured of the confidentiality of services. Children are also recruited as depopulation activists with pitches informing them, as in the widely-used text *Meeting Yourself Halfway:*

"The population problem is very serious and involves every country on this planet. What steps would you encourage to help resolve the problem?

"...volunteer to organize birth-control information centers throughout the country;

"...join a pro-abortion lobbying group;

"...encourage the limitation of two children per family and have the parents sterilized to prevent future births."

Much of sex education literature portrays the nuclear family -- long a cohesive political and social glue among the populace - as obsolete and statistically insignificant, while the normalcy of homosexuality and bachelorism ("Playboyism") is stressed. Children are encouraged to report in detail on conditions at home, to report parental shortcomings, and to divulge disagreements they have with their parents, opening the door to intervention by "social services."

Davis in *Economic Development and Cultural Change* says that an effective strategy in lowering the birth rate is to "lessen... the identity of children with parents, or lessen... the likelihood that this identity will be satisfying," adding that certain trends that might bring population levels down are "very high divorce rates, homosexuality, pornography and free sexual unions..." Davis sees a positive note in "the child welfare services, which have increasingly tended to displace the father as a necessary member of the family, and the health services which have increasingly flouted parental authority with respect to contraception and abortion." This "flouting of parental authority" is a familiar theme in sex education classes, which repeatedly emphasize the child's independence from their parents and their ability to make decisions for themselves.

The message to children, provided by proponents of sex education without the courtesy of having the parents agree upon it, is obvious: the world is awash in excess poor population, and something has to be done about it in a hurry, starting at the nearest abortion clinic.

Educator John Taylor Gatto, voted New York's Top Teacher of 1991, further comments on the mechanism:

"Social machinery to suppress proliferation of systematic families... has two components: one, a campaign aimed at family-formation before it commences, employing such tactics as encouragement of personal greed (best enjoyed in bachelor style, of course), public pornographic celebrations of the body parts of nubile young women, effortless divorce, mass adoption, tolerance of sexual ambiguity, and many similar tactics. The second componant aims at producing pseudo-families: small households (whether biologic or synthetic) without any overriding loyalty to the common family cause. Instead, these are associations of expedience wearing the costume of affection and concern, but always on the lookout for a better deal... During the childhood phase, parents in pseudo-families are made use of by the state to transmit certain values, to maintain and discipline a new serf class composed of their own children, and to report radical cases of deviance to medical, police and re-training authorities... It is a system infused in many places with such black genius in understanding crowd control it is hard not to stand in awe of its unseen architects."

Target populations for sterilization in the United States bear noting. According to Michael Garrity in *Trilateralism*, edited by Holly Sklar, American Indian women are being sterilized unbeknownst to them or against their wishes in public health clinics nationwide. Garrity also maintains, "Full blooded Indian women are the special target of the doctors."

Ruthann Evanoff, in "Reproductive Rights and Occupational Health" in *WIN*, has said that, "Overall, at least 25 percent of the Native women of childbearing age have been sterilized, although the total population numbers less than one million. Recent reports estimate that the percentage sterilized in one tribe alone, the Northern Cheyenne, is close to 80 percent."

The secret (now declassified) paper NSSM 200, "Implications of Worldwide Population Growth For U.S. Security and Overseas Interests," also known as the Scowcroft Document (authored by the CFR's Brent Scowcroft), gives insight into U.S. government plans for population reduction internationally, linking these plans to goals that have very little to do with alleviating human suffering, and everything to do with the maximization of profit.

Prepared in 1974 for the National Security Council (and remember, this is a government document, although one not likely to be offered for free in late night Public Service Announcements) NSSM 200 proposes means for the reduction of worldwide population by "concentration on key [i.e. Third World] countries," with the stated goal of reduction of population growth rate from an annual 2 percent growth to 1.7 percent.

While this might sound like an altruistic goal proposed by clear-sighted social stewards, intended to reduce suffering in countries with marginal standards of living, the study makes it clear that government interest in depopulation has nothing to do with concern for living standards in developing countries. It is because "The United States has become increasingly dependent on mineral imports from developing countries" and "endemic famine, food riots, and breakdown of social order... are scarcely conducive to systematic exploration for mineral deposits or the long-term investments necessary for their exploitation." Note that the breakdown of "social order" referred to consists of the populace revolting against their living conditions.

One of the conclusions of the study is that "*mandatory* [emphasis added] population control measures" may be "appropriate."

Speaking of depopulation programs currently being implemented in the Third World, former Brazilian health minister Carlos Santana said, "The World Bank, through the reports of its Presidents, has always made its proselytizing for a rigid birth control policy explicit." Santana reported that included in World Bank credit packages and investment in Third World countries is an implicit agenda of depopulation, and questioned why Brazil was targeted for birth reduction, with approximately forty per cent of Brazilian women having been already sterilized.

What the depopulators omit saying is that in Brazil most of the depopulation programs are being directed toward the native population, and that they are implementing an alternative program to the *pistoleiros* hired to attack small landowning families, appropriating the land for the use of large cash-croppers and the international conglomerates that are stripping the country bare.

Depopulation programs run worldwide are directed and funded by major international money interests, including McGeorge Bundy of the CFR, the architect of nuclear Mutual Assured Destruction policy; Warren E. Buffett, the second wealthiest man in the United States; and, ubiquitous when it comes to eugenics funding, the Rockefellers.

Planned Parenthood Federation of America and International Planned Parenthood Federation are Buffett-funded and run a huge abortion and sterilization network worldwide, with one subsidiary, the Brazilian Society for Family Welfare, having over 2,500 outlets in that country.

While, at first glance depopulation programs may seem like a good idea to promote the reduction of mouths-to-feed worldwide, what they ignore are the root causes of overpopulation. High birth rates are the direct result of poor living standards of the areas, and in countries where malnutrition has been reduced and the incidence of child-death lowered, birth rates have also lessened. The Third World (in particular) is being forcefully relieved of natural resources and exploited for cheap labor, and is in fact no doubt seen by elite landowners and major corporations as only maintaining maximum profitability as long as it is kept in abject poverty.

"The strategy of underdevelopment" is the term used by agricultural economist Harry Cleaver. Rather than offering the people in countries such as Brazil, in actuality one of the richest countries in the world, an equitable portion of profits made through the use of their resources, they are manipulated (when not killed outright) and kept at the razor edge between starvation and profitability.

Depopulation organizations propagandize that we are experiencing a crisis of epic proportions; that the world is reaching the point where it can no longer support the number of people living on it. In many instances economists, however, doubt this conclusion, suggesting that an increase in population may in fact be economically beneficial, and tending to a long-term increase of arable land and per capita (rather than per corporation) income. Also noted is a current usage of approximately three-tenths of one percent of the planet's surface for human habitation, an amount sustainable with no limit to growth in sight.

United Nations and U.S. Department of Agriculture statistics show that world food production has increased more rapidly than population growth in recent years, while Colin Clark, former director of the Agricultural Economic Institute of Oxford University has stated that farmers could currently support seven times the current population of the Earth, or twenty-one times the current population at Japanese standards of food consumption.

Roger Revelle, former director of the Harvard Center for Population Studies estimates that current agricultural resources could provide an adequate diet for eight times the current populace, i.e. forty billion individuals, and has estimated that Africa is capable of feeding ten times its current population. Revelle quotes Dr. David Hopper, another agricultural expert:

"The world's food problem does not arise from any physical limitation on potential output or any danger of unduly stressing the environment. The limitations on abundance are to be found in the social and political structures of nations and in the economic relations among them. The unexploited global food resource is there, between Cancer and Capricorn. The successful husbandry of that resource depends on the will and actions of men." Hopper pronounces "world fascism" very politely.

Francis Moore Lappe of the Institute for Food and Development Policy maintains:

"If the cause of hunger is neither scarcity of food, nor scarcity of land, we've come to see that it's a scarcity of democracy. That may sound rather contrived, because in the West we tend to think of democracy as a political concept and not as an economic concept. But democracy is really a principle of accountability; in other words, those making the decisions must be accountable to those who are affected by them. Once we understand hunger as a scarcity of democracy, what we are saying is that from the village level to the level of international commerce, fewer and fewer people are making decisions, and more and more anti-democratic structures are being entrenched. This is the cause of hunger." And, it should be repeated, the cause of overpopulation.

12

A Modest Proposal

*T*he early and highly influential eugenicist and Round Tabler George Bernard Shaw offered a modest proposal in 1951:

"If a Black Death could spread throughout the world once in every generation, survivors could procreate freely without making the world too full... The state of affairs might be somewhat unpleasant, but what of it?"

Substantial evidence exists that AIDS was created as a custom-tailored Black Death, although nary a word of such a suspicion appears in the mainstream press.

In 1969, in testimony before the House Appropriations Committee of the U.S. Congress, the Department of Defense's Biological Warfare Division requested $10 million to produce organisms that would selectively destroy the immune system. Quoting from the Committee's minutes, "Within the next 5 to 10 years it would probably be possible to make a new infective microorganism which could differ in certain important respects from any known disease-causing organisms. Most important of these is that it might be refractory to the immunological and therapeutic processes upon which we depend to maintain our relative freedom from infectious disease."

The requested funds were appropriated.

Also in 1969, a portion of the Army's Fort Detrick Biological Warfare Laboratory was transformed into the Frederick Cancer Research Facility and given to, supposedly, the National Cancer Institute for civilian research. "Within two years of its foundation," according to *Covert Action Information Bulletin,* "the Institute's staff and budget had trebled."

In 1972, in volume 47 of the *Bulletin of the World Health Organization,* there was a request by members of that group to make a virus that would selectively destroy the T cell system. "An attempt should be made to ascertain whether viruses can in fact exert selective effects on immune function, e.g. by... affecting T cell function as opposed to B cell function. The possibility should also be looked into that the immune response to the virus itself may be impaired if the infecting virus damages more or less selectively the cells responding to the viral antigens."

In *Federation Proceedings* of the WHO that same year, it was remarked that "we would test these agents that we make by putting it in our vaccines and see what kind of effects they have."

A disease corresponding to the requested characteristics, which we know today as AIDS, did appear within the stipulated period of time. Dr. Robert Strecker reports that the disease appeared in Africa in precisely the same locales that the WHO group said they planned to administer vaccines, and this is supported by an article in the *London Times* for May 11, 1987.

Researcher Waves Forest, in his article "Designer Diseases: AIDS as Biological and Psychological Warfare" writes that, "The AIDS epidemic emerged full-blown in the three U.S cities with 'organized gay communities' before being reported elsewhere, including Haiti or Africa, so it is epidemiologically impossible for either of those countries to be the origin point for the U.S. infections.

"Another indication that AIDS had multiple origin points is that the 14-month doubling time of the disease cannot nearly account for the current number of cases if we assume only a small number of initial infections starting in the late 1970s."

Dr. Strecker relates that AIDS experts have written that "the AIDS virus consists of genes that are related to two known retro-viruses of animals. One is a virus named bovine leukemia, another is a virus named visna." Yet, he points out, these same specialists claim there is no way that these two viruses could have been spliced together.

Dr. Strecker and Dr. Allan Cantwell, testing the claim, went to a medical library and asked the computer to show any available articles on a virus named — taking a wild guess: bovine visna — and, "bang!," they said, "out came articles describing a virus identical to the AIDS virus."

"It had the same morphology (shape), the same molecular weight, the same magnesium dependency, it has the same ability to kill cells, it has the same T cell tropism (it attacks T cells), it has the same exact characteristics in cattle that AIDS does in humans. It produced a disease in cows, characterized by initial lymphomamphy within a few weeks of initial infection, followed by the production of antibodies against that virus, and subsequently, 5-7 years later, the cows died of a wasting disease — and immune deficiency."

Quoting Waves Forest again, "Apparently, homosexuals were an initial target in the U.S. because their sexual practices would help in the rapid spread of the disease, and because it was correctly assumed that very few non-homosexual citizens would pay much attention during the early years of the epidemic. Also, the stigma of 'homosexual disease' would interfere with a rational analysis and discussion of AIDS."

A chilling development in the continuing AIDS controversy was reported in The *Santa Monica Outlook* for December 14, 1989. The RAND Corporation, a CIA-funded organization which will be mentioned again in these pages, issued a warning about the nastiest computer 'virus' yet unleashed upon computer users. The virus had been incorporated, by persons unknown, into a computer disk providing a database for AIDS information. Once let loose in a computer system, it erased every file on AIDS.

Ann Shohen of RAND said workers in AIDS research might have their databases totally destroyed by the virus, and it could infect any computer system networking with such researchers.

John McAfee, chairman of Computer Virus Association, a Santa Monica firm developing anti-virus programs, described the contaminated AIDS disk as part of "a well-orchestrated and undeniably well-financed terrorist act."

Regardless of whether the AIDS epidemic is man-made, regardless of whether the RAND Corporation is covering its own tracks in the interest of plausible denial, this computer virus seems to fit the agendas of certain elitist interests and could well be evidence of continuing efforts to keep AIDS on target in plans for world depopulation.

13

Veins and Tributaries

Another method of genocide and mind control currently being prac-
ticed is chemical warfare — by drugs — upon the population of the world.
The picture is not the simple "good cops vs. evil heroin pushers in the
schoolyard" equation that the mainstream media would have us believe.

Drug dealing is no new thing, although historical precedents are rarely
examined in understanding the problem.

In 1601 the Jesuits established a mission in Beijing, China, providing
contacts for the Portuguese and later the Dutch to native drug trading
routes in the East, with the Dutch negotiating an opium monopoly for the
northern part of the Indian subcontinent. The British East India Company
established trade in opium and slaves after opening an office in Canton,
China, and when Bengal was made a Crown Colony in 1757 "John Company" expanded its trade in close collaboration with the British crown and
Rothschild bankers. In the 1860 siege of Beijing the British (under the
direction of Prime Minister Lord Palmerston, at the time the world head of
the Scottish Rite of Freemasonry) forced the opening of the drug trade.
Britain's admitted policy of "sapping the vitality" of China via opium trafficking to its population provides an early example of chemical-psychologi-
cal warfare.

After the opening of Chinese ports, the British-owned Hong Kong and
Shanghai Corporation was established, in a policy of breaking British East
India interests into individual and difficult-to-trace assets. The Hong Kong
and Shanghai Bank to this day remains connected to the laundering and
internal flow of international drug monies, with the management of much
of drug financing and shipment allegedly supervised from on high by deni-
zens of the Royal Institute of International Affairs (a front for the Round

Table group) and the British Secret Service. The historical policy of British overlords using drugs to decimate the Chinese culture oddly hearkens to the realities of today.

In America, John Jacob Astor was the first to exploit the lucrative possibilities of Chinese opium, with other Anglophile "Boston Brahmin" families following suit. Prohibition was also planned by these interests, with the Temperance movement financially sponsored by the Astors, Vanderbilts, Rockefellers, and Warburgs, the latter linked to the Rothschilds by marriage.

Prohibition vastly increased the profitability of alcohol and drugs, supplied through British networks with distilleries in Scotland and Canada and opium refineries in Shanghai and Hong Kong. During Prohibition, liquor and drug shipments were supplied by British interests and transported to America via the Canadian Bronfman gang (who have since attained respectability as the owners of Seagrams, America's largest liquor distributor, and by membership in the Knights of Malta) with American distribution performed by the networks of mobsters Arnold Rothstein, Meyer Lansky and Lucky Luciano. The United Fruit Company, owned jointly by the Lansky Mafia and Boston Brahmins, has been identified by American intelligence as historically one of the major transporters of drugs into the United States.

Alfred McCoy in his *The Politics of Heroin* states that at the end of World War II "with American consumer demand reduced to its lowest point in fifty years and the international syndicates in disarray, the U.S. government had a unique opportunity to eliminate heroin addiction as a major American social problem. However, instead of delivering the death-blow to these criminal syndicates, the U.S. Government — through the Central Intelligence Agency and its wartime predecessor, the OSS — created a situation that made it possible for the Sicilian-American Mafia and the Corsican underworld to revive the international narcotics traffic."

What assisted the revival of the heroin traffic in this century was a secret Franklin Roosevelt alliance with the Mafia's Meyer Lansky, providing immunity for Lansky's smuggling operations in exchange for protection of the Eastern seaboard during World War II and, later, in the wresting of control of the French docks from Socialist unions. As part of the deal, Lucky Luciano was released from prison after World War II, and quickly proceeded to set up a base of operations for heroin smuggling in Cuba, later turning over the reins to Santos Trafficante, in Miami.

Elsewhere, in the CIA's support for "Nationalist" China, they supplied Chaiang Kai-Shek's Kuomintang (KMT) with arms and supplies for their stronghold in Burma. There CIA-allied General Phao built up the opium trade as a source of funding the KMT, with arms flown into Burma and opium flown out by the CIA's Air America. In a Congressional investigation of the heroin trade, Joe Nellis stated: "The CIA did help bring some very powerful cheap heroin into Vietnam out of the Shan States, the northern states of Burma... for radio communications, intelligence. In return for that intelligence, the CIA winked at what went in its airplanes."

Air America has hardly been the CIA's only involvement in fostering the international drug trade. The Nugan-Hand Bank was started by CIA agent Michael Jon Hand and employed Dulles colleague General Edwin F. Black, retired CIA Director William Colby, former deputy CIA Director Walter McDonald, and Kissinger and Brzezinski advisor Guy Pauker on its payroll. Nugan-Hand seems to have largely existed through the laundering of drug monies, as a tributary flowing into a central drug laundering connection, the British-owned Hong Kong and Shanghai Bank. Nugan-Hand even had an office located in Chaiang Mai, a rural town in Thailand known as the last outpost for travellers into the "Golden Triangle." Conveniently, the Nugan-Hand office was located in the same office, in the same suite, as the Chaiang Mai branch of the U.S. Drug Enforcement Agency.

The Nugan-Hand Bank was involved in a number of unusual deals, including the financing of the Rhodesian government of Ian Smith, in which 250,000 whites ruled millions of vote-less blacks, and a similar situation in the Portuguese colonial government in Angola. Nugan-Hand also worked with the CIA in the overthrowing by coup d'etat of Australian Prime Minister Gough Whitlam in 1975 — reported by the Australian press to have been done on the instructions of Henry Kissinger.

Although the flow of drugs and drug monies at the retail level is labyrinthine, it proceeds to central hubs. Drug trade is absolutely integrated into and props up international banking, government and secret societies, with clandestine agencies and police forces providing the enforcement and sometimes transportation arms of these operations.

Chase Manhattan's International Advisory Board Chairman Kissinger was the author of the plan to raise international interest rates to 20% in 1979, putting the screws to Ibero American debtors to the International Monetary Fund and encouraging them to change over to a drug economy. The former foreign minister of Guyana, Frederick Wills, described it this way:

"The countries hope that by getting the IMF seal of approval, this will open the gates for credit from other countries and private banks. But the IMF seal of approval requires successful acceptance of the IMF program. And since you didn't succeed, the flow of funds from money markets and banks is dried up. This means that, first of all, the government ministers started to think that, 'What export could we have which could realize quick cash flow, to stem this balance of payments gap?' There is only one commodity that satisfies that requirement: dope, heroin, marijuana."

One discernible link of the drug trade with the U.S. government is the illegal Contra supply operations run by then-Vice President George Bush under National Security Decision Directive 3 during the 1980s. Shipments of guns for the Contras were smuggled by known drug traffickers, who in turn (known or unknown to Bush) brought back thousands of kilos of cocaine to the United States, some of them transported through Homestead Air Force Base near Miami, Florida. If the principals in the operation, people like then-V.P. Bush, Colonel North, Admiral Poindexter, and Major General Secord (also a player in Nugan-Hand) were not receiving a portion of the profits, then it must have been a case of the government "winking at what went into its airplanes."

Notified in many instances of drug trafficking, the Reagan and Bush administrations often acted to block investigations and prosecution. The invasion of Panama, presented to the public as an intervention intended to stop the drug trafficking of world-class outlaw Manuel Noriega, takes on the complexion of a turf war when one learns that George Bush quickly installed Guillermo "Porky" Endara in the Panamanian presidency after Noriega was dethroned. Endara was co-owner, with drug lord Rodriguez Gacha, of the money-laundering Banco Interoceanico, as well as the owner of the ship Sea Point, caught twice in shipments of cocaine and Israeli arms. Installed as President, Attorney General, President of the Supreme Court, and Minister of the Treasury were members on the board of First Interamericas Bank, earlier closed by Noriega after he had received proof that the bank was owned by the Cali Cartel.

The Washington Post has characterized American government actions in Panama as an alliance with the Cali Cartel against the Medellin Cartel. Not as improbable as it might seem when one discovers that the director of the Office of International Affairs of the U.S. Justice Department, Michael Abbell, is reported to be a registered Washington lobbyist for the Cali Cartel.

And since the overthrow and silencing of Noriega, drug trafficking in Panama has only increased.

One will never understand the significance of international drug trafficking unless it is seen for what it is: a major world industry. Drugs are currently the second largest international trading commodity after oil, with an estimated $500 billion dollars in yearly worldwide sales. The necessity of laundering huge amounts of currency at wholesale level makes it highly doubtful that the business is conducted by illiterate Golden Triangle and

Columbian warlords. Billions of dollars in loans to men in drug-growing regions, and the amount of drug monies being laundered through worldwide banking are so large that it is not possible, especially with the availability of modern electronic scanning methods, that the banks involved are unaware of the sources of their funding.

I do not include a list of national banks used as international drug tributaries because it would literally require pages, but these smaller channels pour funds into the monetary oceans of the unregulated "Group of 10" offshore banks, large Bangkok banks (alleged to be the financiers of Golden Triangle operations), expatriate Chinese banks, Rothschild banks, and British banks and trading companies, including the previously-mentioned Hong Kong and Shanghai Bank (overseeing approximately 350 financial institutions in Hong Kong).

The Hong Kong and Shanghai bank is governed by the elite London Committee, with two of its directors former senior officials in Britain's Ministry of Economic Warfare, with other members linked to the Royal Institute of International Affairs. London's part in the concealment of international drug monies can be confirmed by the March 1984 study "Crime and Secrecy: The Use of Offshore Banks and Companies," of the Permanent Investigations Subcommittee of the U.S. Senate, which charges London banking with being the international center for the concealment of drug money.

"And there are other rationales for traffic in drugs," Lanny Sinkin of the Christic Institute has said. "In analyzing the evidence available, the Institute and others concluded that the War on Drugs was not what it appeared. In essence, the United States government facilitated the entry of drugs into this country as part of a larger program. The two major elements of this program are: (1) a real war in Central and South America using the influx of drugs into this country as the rationale and (2) the suppression of domestic populations with the use of drugs and the attendant violence and crime as the rationale."

To paraphrase, there is a war going on worldwide which at one level has nothing to do with drugs, although it can be sold to the public, particularly the American public, on the basis of suppression of drugs. By simultaneously creating anti-drug legislation and fostering drug trade (mirroring the operation that took place in America during Prohibition), international manipulators obtain both a rationalization for that war and for the increased police penetration of society and suppression of political freedoms.

The fundamental game is not traffic in drugs, but the traffic in human lives and energy, the buying, selling and herding of cattle-resources. It boils down to the ultimate master/slave relationship with the masters in a continual struggle for profits and to keep the people uninformed, sated, mindless, utilized. The "host," be it animal, human or planet, is anesthetized, then drained by its parasitic self-styled masters. And then the ravaged hulk is discarded.

14

Emergency Action

*I*t does not take an extensive study of the action of the masters of any age, the pharaohs, the kings, the popes, the Rothschilds, the Rockefellers, to verify their existence or to determine their modus operandi. This ruling class (in its darkest and sometimes hidden manifestations) is unfettered by such insignificant things as ethical or moral qualms. They uniformly view themselves as pure-blooded aristocrats and the minions beneath them in the same way that most people view cattle — as animals to be harvested. This harvesting is usually done by the men ostensibly hired to protect us.

Although the Soviet threat, we are led to believe, has been banished and blown to the winds, there seems to be little likelihood that "our protectors," the American Spy State, will soon wither away and die.

The CIA, since its inception, has run an estimated 3,000 major operations and 10,000 minor operations. Ex-CIA agent John Stockwell has estimated a minimum death toll of six million individuals in the Third World from these operations. Even during the current economic depression (I mean, recession) and amid the crumbling of our cities, American spy and paramilitary operations continue to drain 35 billion documented dollars per year while employing 25,000 individuals in America and untold thousands worldwide through subsidiary networks, companies, and organizational cutouts.

Russ Baker, in the *Village Voice,* has termed the spy establishment "little more than the private army of the Fortune 500," and it is an apt, if limited, description of this enormous, mostly-invisible security force which works with a huge network of ex-spooks and collaborators in actions often designed to violate international law and to trample human rights.

There are more than a dozen government agencies which are in the business of gathering intelligence and covert action, and they are in part funded through "black budget" allocations whose nature is not made available to the Congress, much less the public, but which is currently estimated to be in the same range as their above-board funding. More money is spent on the CIA, the NSA, and their brother agencies than is spent on education in America — and the money is spent on spies.

The Congressional watchdogs seem variously not to care about the actions of the intelligence community, or to be cheering them on and collaborating in the attempts of the wolves to batter down the gates of Constitutional safeguards, and the continued overthrow of constitutional democracies worldwide.

Former aide to the Director of Central Intelligence Victor Marchetti described the process of infiltration of Congress: "They sent up top guns... like John Clark — who had been head of Planning, Programming, and Budgeting in the CIA on the director's staff. The whole idea was to snow these guys, con these guys, win these guys over, convert 'em, get 'em on the team. That's what has happened. It's now institutionalized."

Another reason why Congress and the public are not able to see into the double dealing of the security state is that they are not allowed to glimpse the lion's share of its activities. "We'd go down and lie to them consistently," Ex-CIA man Ralph McGee said of his experiences with Congress. "In my 25 years, I have never seen the agency tell the truth to a congressional committee."

With the Soviet Union gone, there is little doubt that new threats will crop up to replace the KGB and to justify the existence of the spy establishment. The odds-on favorites are terrorism, the drug war, and the shooing into line of whatever Third World (and most likely previously American-sponsored) dictator the press chooses to characterize this week as a latter-day Hitler. Already the CIA has put forth feelers to Congress suggesting that a new threat looms large on the post-USSR horizon: industrial and economic sabotage by competing countries.

Many of the underlying theoretical threads of *Alternative 3* come together when we examine one room among many in the "mansion" of U.S. intelligence, the Federal Emergency Management Agency. The first inklings of FEMA surfaced in 1969, when California governor Ronald Reagan instituted a special training project at the National Guard Camp in San Luis Obispo, California. The purpose of the seminar was to train leaders in population control. A fictional town of "San Luisa" was mapped and broken into ethnic and income zones, and plans for infiltration of groups and methods for crowd control were formulated. By 1979 the *Associated*

Press reported that 14,000 persons had been trained in this population control seminar.

FEMA proper was created by Jimmy Carter. Housed in one of the government's tightest security installations and located in Fort Meade, Maryland, FEMA is currently computerizing records on millions of Americans, preparing a database for CAPs, Crisis Action Programs to be utilized in the event of whatever the Executive Department might term a national crisis.

Incorporating the disaster and emergency functions of a dozen different federal agencies, FEMA has concentrated on such activities as plans for setting up mass emergency detention centers in case anything might threaten the "continuity of government" (COG). As Dr. Henry Kleinmann, a political scientist at Boston University, said: "It was understood that they [FEMA]... would one day be in charge of the country. As these bureaucrats saw it, FEMA's real mission was to wait, prepare and then take over when some 'situation' seemed serious enough to turn the United States into a police state."

The intervention of FEMA on a national scale would not require a massive ecological disaster, but, in the words of Executive Order 11921, it could be utilized "whenever necessary for assuring the continuity of the federal government in any national emergency type situation." A congressional investigation in 1991 showed that less than 10 percent of FEMA's staff of 2,600 bureaucrats are preparing for a cataclysmic natural event. So what is FEMA preparing for?

One answer can be read in Presidential Executive Order EO 12656 issued by President Ronald Reagan on November 18, 1988, which defined a National Emergency (such as would activate FEMA) as "any occurrence, including natural disaster, military attack, technological emergency or other emergency, that seriously degrades or seriously threatens the national security of the United States." That pretty well covers all possible bases. Any event, then, which can be construed as threatening to the government can be used to set a host of repressive Executive Orders into action, including:

- EO 10995, authorizing the suspension of the freedom of speech and the commandeering of all of the communications media.
- EO 10997, authorizing the takeover of electrical systems and other fuel sources.
- EO 10998, providing for the government control of food sources, including farms.
- EO 10999, which authorizes the control or confiscation of the nation's transportation sources, public and private.

- EO 11000, which gives government the right to form work brigades of citizens.

- EO 11001, providing for the takeover of all health, education, and welfare functions and facilities.

- EO 11002, authorizing a national registering of the populace.

- EO 11003, authorizing the takeover of all airplanes and airports.

- EO 11004, which gives government the mandate to relocate populations from one area to another.

- EO 11005, which provides for government to take over railways, waterways, and public storage facilities.

- EO 12148, authorizing FEMA to take over the executive functions of the government.

These Executive Orders have all been recorded in the Federal Register, and accepted by Congress as law. They can be put into effect any time an emergency is declared. The above EOs were incorporated into one Executive Order (EO 11490) by President Richard Nixon and, further, Jimmy Carter's 1979 Executive Orders creating FEMA delegated to it the power to act for the President.

These orders are a few of the legal justifications available to the unelected bureaucrats at FEMA and their masters, which can be used for widespread repression and the complete suspension of Constitutional rights in the event of anything deemed a national emergency.

During the Iran-Contra hearings of 1987, there was a telling exchange between Representative Jack Brooks and Senator Daniel Inouye:

"Brooks: Colonel North, in your work at the N.S.C. [National Security Council, which is also the location of FEMA], were you not assigned, at one time, to work on plans for the continuity of government in the event of a major disaster?

Brendan Sullivan (North's counsel): Mr. Chairman?

Senator Daniel Inouye: I believe that question touches upon a highly sensitive and classified area so may I request that you not touch upon that?

Representative Brooks: I was particularly concerned, Mr. Chairman, because I read in the Miami papers, and several others, that there had been a plan developed, by that same agency, a contingency plan in the event of emergency, that would suspend the American Constitution. And I was deeply concerned about it and wondered if that was the area in which he had worked. I believe that it was and I wanted to get his confirmation.

Senator Inouye: May I most respectfully request that matter not be touched upon, at this stage. If we wish to get into this, I'm certain arrangements can be made for an executive session."

With the rampant excesses of the American intelligence community and agencies such as FEMA, the means for the implementation of *Alternative 3* or similar plans are in place, and whether EO 11004 is invoked to usher us off to the moon, Mars, or merely to an American Gulag, it seems quite irrelevant.

15

Demonstration Project

*I*n Oracle, Arizona exists what has been touted as a self-contained Earth: Biosphere II, a huge three-acre, ten-story geodesic structure supporting 40,000 plants and eight "crew members" who plan to exist isolated from the outside world for two years. After six years of planning and an investment of $100 million dollars, *Discover* magazine has called Biosphere II "the most exciting scientific project to be undertaken in the U.S. since President Kennedy launched us toward the moon."

Among the collaborators on Biosphere II are the Smithsonian Institute, the National Center for Atmospheric Research, the Yale School of Forestry and Ecological Science, The New York Botanical Gardens, the University of Arizona's Environmental Research Laboratory, the U.S. Geological Society, and NASA.

Biosphere has been portrayed in glowing terms on all the major television networks, in the *New York Times*, the *Los Angeles Times*, *The Boston Globe*, *The Washington Post*, *Omni*, and *National Geographic World*. Hosting an hour-long show from the Arizona site, Phil Donahue called it "one of the most ambitious man-made projects ever." In other words, establishment science and the media have bought wholeheartedly (if that is the correct term) into the project. But the veneer of scientific and media respectability do more to reinforce our understanding of science as the whore of the controllers than it does to assuage our doubts about the validity or purpose of Biosphere II.

The Biosphere project was founded in the 1980s by John P. Allen (aka "Johnny Dolphin"), and funded by Allen follower and Texas millionaire Edward P. Bass. Bass' money enabled Allen to transform a small apocalyptic religious group living in a desert commune in Santa Fe, New Mexico into the darlings of the media and scientific establishment. Among properties owned by Allen and his group are a Katmandu hotel, a ranch in Australia of several thousand acres, a conference center in France, and a theater-cultural center in Fort Worth, Texas.

University of California professor Laurence Vesey spent five weeks researching John Allen's commune, known as Synergia Ranch, in the early 70s. His observations, published in a book called *The Communal Experience,* provide a somewhat different image than the scientific jargon and coral-red jumpsuits that the members of Allen's group affect today.

Veysey found an experiment in progress that was, according to him, "Jonestown-like," and geared to Allen's vision of a dying Earth that could only be saved by founding a new civilization... on Mars.

Allen told Vesey: "Western civilization isn't simply dying. It's dead." Synergia, he said, was "poking among the ruins of the dying civilization in order to snatch whatever is currently of service to the new."

Vesey described Allen as having "total hold and domination" over his group of followers. "The others all look to him constantly for their cues, for the subtle signals which tell them what to do and what not to do... His chanting rhythm they imitate with their own voices, his instructions they seek to apply in the theater [they employ], his timetable they follow for planetary outreach... [Allen's] domination over the group is open and for the most part undisguised... This entire societal order is the tangible enactment of his own vision."

Vesey said that Allen's warnings of ecological and atomic destruction were continually ranted at the members of the commune, and that Geiger counters had been purchased for his followers, presumably for use during the event of atomic war.

Speaking of nightly group psychological confrontations, Vesey said that Allen would ask: "Any confessions?" If there were no volunteers, Allen "will explode into wrath, usually directed at one person. Calmly in control of himself one minute, in the next he will be shouting the most hurtful words conceivable in a furious assault upon the ego of some trapped individual... He will seize upon what appear to be innocent failures to follow precise instructions and transform them into calculated acts of sabotage... He reiterates his accusations until no possible response is left. Then, all at once, his tirade comes to an end and everyone continues as if nothing had happened."

Vesey recently spoke of Biosphere II, saying that it "has all kinds of implications... the Biosphere is a demonstration project that fits in with the political thinking of the right wing. A more liberal kind of person might wonder why you should sink all that money into something for the survival of only a few people." Vesey says that Allen believes that he is gathering together a new "elite" for the purpose of constructing a "new civilization," yet is "masking it" from the uninitiated.

Researcher Wade Davis recently spent time with the Biosphere group. He described the project as having an atmosphere of "oppressive... almost totalitarian... hippie fascism. Most importantly they seem to have no knowledge nor interest in botany," which research is one of the expressed purposes of Biosphere II.

Television producer Ed Fitzgerald said of his time at Biosphere II, "The whole experience was marked by a feel of paranoia. The critics we talked to demanded meetings in open places, public parks. We had to ask ourselves several times if we just felt we were being followed or if we were."

An account published in the *Village Voice* described a visit to Biosphere II: "Once a visit to the dome has been secured, you might as well be in Baghdad. All interviews are conducted in the presence of a PR 'minder,' who, with watch and walkie-talkie in hand, makes sure no chat becomes too intimate, or probes too closely about who these people are in their off hours. In fact, all questions about the personal lives of the Biospherians are taboo. It is no accident that of the dozens of published accounts on the project — all sympathetic — not one describes the family, friends, or homes of the Biosphere crew or management. The few who are authorized to speak to the press are almost all core group members. With no attempt at exaggeration or interpretation, let it be said they are almost uniformly humorless. As cold as the fish in their artificial ocean. Not a crack of human frailty or emotion is revealed. The answers that are given are rote and flat in tone, worlds away from the hyperpoetry of their promotional brochures."

Describing the tenets in the group's major promotional tract, the *Voice* author said, "And it is a dark religion. In its introductory chapter, the pamphlet openly declares: 'the major motivation behind creating Biosphere II and developing the capacity to create other microscale viable biospheric systems is to assist the Biosphere [i.e. the lifeforms of Earth] to evolve off planet Earth into potential life regions of our solar system.'"

The last third of the book emphasizes the "historic imperative" of colonizing Mars, given the "inevitable doom" of the Earth, which is described as a "local blind alley" and estimates that work on the Mars project will begin in approximately four years. A book of Allen's poetry on sale in the Biosphere gift shop includes a poem, titled (in perhaps telling fashion) "*Lebensraum*," about his plot to escape this planetary "cell."

As to whether Allen read *Alternative 3* and thought it was a bright idea, or whether he happens to be a front-man for a group using Biosphere II as a test tube for social experimentation (which may have been the case in Jonestown), I have no idea. Regardless, there can hardly be a better clue than these gleaming geodesic structures in the Arizona desert that there exist men proposing to abandon Earth, forging new schemes of mind control off-planet.

16

Lunar Base Alpha One

*D*eceased conspiracy researcher Dr. Peter Beter is known for his wild speculations (including the insistence that Jimmy Carter, Henry Kissinger, David Rockefeller and Leonid Brezhnev were replaced by "organic robotoids" — would that it were so). Beter believed *Alternative 3* was about "85 to 90 percent accurate."

Acknowledging a blur between fiction and fact in *Alternative 3*, I present Beter's story of the Battle of Harvest Moon, knowing full well that it is probably fictional in most details, but interesting in the parallels it presents with *Alternative 3* — and *Alternative 3* is nothing if not a study in parallels.

In Beter's *Audio Letter* for September 1977, in his inimitable "Criswell Predicts" style, he relates the American and Russian space programs' true objectives. According to Beter, these programs have always been militaristic in purpose and secretly intended for conquest of the world, with their key components being the development of laser and particle beam weapons.

The Rockefellers, the true power behind American politics according to Beter, had early realized that a moon base equipped with laser could strike any spot on Earth and be virtually immune to counterattack. A secret American space program was initiated, and work on U.S. beam weapons proceeded at locations such as a CIA installation in Spain. Meanwhile, the USSR concentrated on its own particle beam program instead of moon flight. In 1972 the Russian civil defense program was stepped up and much of the Soviet Union, including strategic command centers, went underground in order to withstand ICBMs and particle beams.

In 1973, according to Beter, the Americans relocated all native inhabitants from Diego Garcia, an island in the Indian Ocean, and built a new space port from which secret missions to the moon were launched in order to build a base there. Diego Garcia is very isolated, and craft launched eastward pass over a nearly unbroken expanse of water, with the only means of monitoring such launches being from shipboard. Jimmy Carter gave a speech about demilitarizing the Indian Ocean, with the implicit message to the Russians, according to Beter, to stay out.

Meanwhile, the CIA was busy planting supermissiles using Howard Hughes' submarine Glomar Explorer. With this episode, also reported by Bruce Roberts in his underground *Gemstone File*, Beter may be correct. In "The Secret Alliances of the CIA from World War II to Watergate" by Howard Kohn, published in *Rolling Stone* magazine, Kohn says: "Many CIA experts believe the Russian sub story [using the Glomar Explorer to retrieve the sunken submarine] to be a cover since the codes were outdated and the value of the other information was negligible. One possibility is that the CIA, worried about the growing trend of Third World cartels demanding higher prices for minerals, awarded Hughes the $350 million to develop an advanced technology for underwater mining — thereby giving Hughes a head start toward a bonanza with more potential than oil while helping protect U.S. hegemony over the world's mineral trade. Another theory is that the CIA, in conjunction with the U.S. Navy, used the Glomar to set up undetected missile sites on the ocean floor as a way of cheating any arms limitation treaty with the Soviet Union."

The race for an operational particle beam continued, so Beter says, with the Russian Salyud spacecraft carrying out beam tests in space. On July 17, 1973, the Russian Cosmos 929 was launched, consisting of a twin satellite, command module, and a particle beam module. All communications between the Cosmos 929 and Earth were carried on by undetectable modulated laser beams. Meanwhile, in the Copernicus crater base on the moon, the Americans were working toward operational status for their beam weapons.

Cosmos 929 began test firing into open space. On September 20, 1977 the Cosmos fired on an American spy satellite east of southern Finland. The satellite erupted into a fireball witnessed, according to Beter, as far away as Helsinki but dismissed as a UFO in the U.S. British and French trawlers were expelled from the Bering Sea by the Russians and on September 26th, 1977 the Soviets attacked the moon base with particle beams. Bombarded by beam weapons through the night and all day of the 27th, by evening America had lost the battle.

The moon base, in the Beter scenario, had been integral to the Rockefeller plot to control the world. Their plan was to start a limited nuclear war, most of the destruction to take place on American soil. The plan was to denude America of war capability while building up the Soviets. With half of America incinerated by bombs the Rockefellers would step in with the moon base's particle beam weapons and destroy the U.S.S.R., then, as the only remaining major power, the Rockefellers would be enthroned as dictators.

After the Battle of the Harvest Moon, Gromyko gave, according to Beter, an ultimatum in a United Nations speech... as the Bering Sea filled up with Soviet subs. The Soviet's North Atlantic and Pacific fleets were massing and six more particle beam satellites were readied for launch, with two in orbit already.

Gromyko denounced the deterioration of East/West relations and demanded a new agreement for the limitation of nuclear weapons. In a meeting with Carter and Vance, Gromyko informed them of the outcome of Harvest Moon, saying that the U.S.S.R. had destroyed the American moon base and was now in command. "We will oblige you with the war you have worked to bring about."

The following day Soviet submarine fleets armed with neutron bombs converged from positions worldwide, and the Soviets placed sixty cobalt bombs at undersea fracture zones worldwide, able to set off earthquakes at will. In a news conference Carter blurted out something about the "imminent" crises.

Within days an American Atlas Centaur rocket carrying an important communications satellite exploded. Salyud 6 was launched and the Soviets went to work on their own moon base, with the intention of putting a particle beam weapon on the moon. Houston NASA moon base activities shut down.

Dr. Beter concluded his message of September 1977 by stating that war was virtually upon us.

While Beter's story seems highly unlikely given the events of the breakup of the Soviet Union, I note that many elements closely parallel *Alternative 3* and that Beter came to the same conclusion I had reached in regard to the death of the SDI scientists: that the Russians would have seen the program's offensive capabilities and would have been forced into a strategy to prevent its completion. As far as his insistence that the Americans had a base on the moon, I can only state that the base does exist — but perhaps only in terms of plans.

Beter's scenario might also explain the otherwise odd initial emphasis of the American space program on reaching the moon. If the moon flight was accomplished in the manner that NASA made public, it would have would have resulted in only a PR triumph, with the Soviets at the same time "content" to emphasize in their own programs rockets capable of carrying huge cargos and orbiting stations with unknown payloads.

In March 1965 General Thomas M. Power warned of the possibility of attack by orbiting Russian nuclear stations. He said that Americans "may wake up one morning" and find nuclear-armed satellites "floating in stationary orbits over every part of the United States."

In 1981 *Aviation Week* and CBS News reported that there were permanent Russian space platforms armed with killer satellites orbiting the Earth. The Pentagon chose not to comment on the reports.

Space Age Review for November 1981 reported that the United States had developed a "U.S. Space Command" to "meet the needs of the Pentagon's war preparations," also stating that the U.S. was knowingly breaking the 1967 Russian-American space treaty, which prohibits "placing in orbit around the Earth any objects carrying nuclear weapons or other weapons of mass destruction."

Another echo of Beter's scenario is information I received from an anonymous intelligence source in 1991, later confirmed through an independent source in the military. I am not suggesting that the report is absolutely true, only that independent confirmation makes it more likely to be so.

My informant said: "I do know that the U.S. has had an orbiting nuclear weapons platform for at least the past twenty years; enough straight nukes to do all the damage necessary, plus two that are cobalt-jacketed. One of these, dropped on Peking, would spread fallout as far east as Utah. These were part of the old Standard Integrated Operational Plan (SIOP) coded 'Endgame'; the straight nukes were part of the SIOP coded 'Mainchance.' I also know that the first military-run shuttle mission was sent up to service the platform and upgrade the on-board computers. The platform's capabilities were most likely enhanced by this upgrading, though I don't think the weapons were changed at all. There may actually be more than one platform by now, but one is all they need — especially since it could just as easily be used on domestic targets... Add that to the spate of new surveillance satellites they've put up, entirely too many in geo-synchronous orbit over the U.S. and its territories, and it's no surprise that people like myself are paranoid..."

Bill Kaysing, former employee of NASA, also backs up Beter's scenario in a number of details, but believes the moon base was eventually phased out: "...As most aerospace insiders know, the Apollo project was actually a military mission to determine the feasibility of using the moon as a military base of operations against foreign powers. Furthermore, almost 75 percent of all NASA effort was basically military — not space!

"When the capability of controlling orbiting H-bombs became a reality, the moon became far less important to the Pentagon's planners. Who needs a moon base when it's possible to destroy any or all of the planet with bombs disguised as communications satellites that orbit the Earth 24 hours a day, they reasoned."

The make-or-break point on a moon base or a "black" space race is ultimately financial, it would seem, and it is really a question of whether there was a sufficient military black budget to finance such activities — which, however, could have been done on the relative cheap by utilizing the researches and perhaps diverting some of the money allocated to NASA. The objection that a project of such a magnitude could not go on without information leaking to the press is probably false. The Manhattan Project, for instance, employed more than 300,000 persons, and yet no significant leaks appeared in the press at the time.

In an interview conducted by researcher Thomas Lyttle, agricultural expert Richard Miller spoke of his employment in an outer space hydroponics research project from 1968-72 under the administration of Dr. Arthur Pilgrim. Funded by a major aeronautics company in the Northwest, the researches were "for use on the moon. This project was called Lunar Base Alpha One Project... We were part of a study at one point on zero gravity. McCormick Foods [a company connected to the Rockefellers] had an overrun of something like seventeen million dollars that they needed to reinvest, so they formed what was called McCor/Shill or McCormick's/Shilling Platform. These were the people who did experiments with orbiting space platforms - orbiting satellites, etc. These were all secret biological experiments." Note that Miller uses the same terminology used in the account of the anonymous informant: "platform."

Brian O'Leary, the first astronaut to resign from NASA, also spoke about a secret space program in his book *The Making of an Ex-Astronaut*:

"The Air Force also has a center at Cape Kennedy, fending independently from NASA with its own gantries and its own... VIB, the Vehicle Installation Building. These facilities sit on landfill adjacent to Merritt Island, isolated from the NASA structures. We toured the Air Force center but learned little about their highly secret space program. Many people do not realize that the world has three ambitious manned space programs: the U.S. (NASA), Russia, and the U.S. Air Force. The Air Force space program operates under the protection of secrecy offered by the military, in contrast to NASA's exposure to public scrutiny. We probably know less about our Air Force space program than we do about the Soviet space program. We do know a few things, though. They have the Titan III (very difficult to hide), a big tricylinder rocket which looks like a multiple firecracker. The two extra cylinders were strapped on as an afterthought, and the three together deliver a strong thrust which is intermediate between those of the Saturn IB and Saturn V.

"Our tour of the Air Force facility seemed like a broken record: the computers, the consoles, and the rockets were similar to NASA's and it struck me that the whole thing was an unnecessary duplication. Imagine — two independent but similar programs going on at the same site. The Air Force space program seemed like a foreign space program, except we were spending dearly for it."

O'Leary also refers to future space prospects, in a comment that makes me wonder if he is indulging an arch humor: "A manned Mars landing may be in prospect for the 1980s or 1990s. President Nixon's appointed Space Task Group outlined *three alternatives* [emphasis added], all of which would involve the Mars landing before the end of the century..."

What if, as *Alternative 3* suggests, there is a moon or Mars base already in operation? Then there may have been indications of its existence. Curious lights, clouds, and unexplainable moving objects on the surface of the moon have been observed by both professional and amateur astronomers, and Fred Steckling's *Alien Bases on the Moon* offers a remarkable assortment of photographs of inexplicable Lunar features. These include large objects which seem to have travelled across the Lunar landscape, leaving miles of stitch-like paths; what appear to be Arabic numerals and other symbols carved into the lunar surface in conjunction with dome-like objects; and multiple triangular pond-like constructions which utterly defy any explanation as natural formations.

An AP news story featured an interview with Michael Carr, a member of the team interpreting photographs of Mars sent back to Earth from the Viking 2 orbiter. Carr said: "We are getting some strange things. It is very puzzling." Carr explained that some of the photographs of the Martian surface showed features resembling agricultural strip plowing. "The stripes are too regular to be of natural causes." As to what the research team thought the striped area was, Carr said: "I really can't tell you all of the possibilities that were suggested. But many suggestions were that it was MAN MADE." Note that Carr doesn't term the features "alien made."

There are reports that the astronauts encountered strange things on the moon whose existence was never revealed to the public. The book *Alternative 3* repeats author Otto Binder's assertion that during the Apollo 11 mission this exchange took place over the radio:

Mission Control: "What's there?... malfunction (garble)... Mission Control calling Apollo 11..."

Apollo 11: "These babies were huge, sir... enormous... Oh, God you wouldn't believe it!... I'm telling you there are other space-craft out there... lined up on the far side of the crater edge... they're on the Moon watching us..."

My initial impulse was to discount this alleged bit of radio communication, based as it is solely on the word of Otto Binder (who, in collaboration with his brother Edward, was half of the science fiction writing team Eando Binder). I might also have been negatively influenced by the numerous patently fake transcripts of other secret conversations between "conspirators" in the book *Alternative 3*. Timothy Good, however, relates a tale told to him by "a certain professor (whose name is known to me)... who served in British military intelligence." Good says that the professor recollects a conversation with Neil Armstrong which took place during a NASA symposium:

PROFESSOR:" What really happened out there with Apollo 11?"

ARMSTRONG: "It was incredible... of course, we had always known there was a possibility... the fact is, we were warned off. There was never any question then of a space station or a moon city."

PROFESSOR: "What do you mean 'warned off?'"

ARMSTRONG: "I can't go into details, except to say that their ships were far superior to ours both in size and technology — Boy, they were big!... and menacing... No, there is no question of a space station."

PROFESSOR: "But NASA had other missions after Apollo 11?"

ARMSTRONG: "Naturally — NASA was committed at that time, and couldn't risk a panic on Earth... But it really was a quick scoop and back again."

Armstrong, not surprisingly, denies the story.

An incredible objectification of *Alternative 3* exists in the book *Space Settlements, A Design Study,* edited by Johnson and Holbrow (NASA document SP-413). Authored by participants in the 1975 Summer faculty fellowship program in engineering systems design of Ames Research Center and Stanford University, and sponsored by NASA, the book analyzes from an engineering perspective the requirements necessary to launch and maintain extraterrestrial colonies, but oddly presents much of its text in present tense, as if the reader was a participant in an already-existing program.

Viewed from the perspective of the *Alternative 3* allegations numerous portions of the book will provoke a sense of recognition, if not dread. From a section titled "Tour of the Colony."

"Preparation for your trip is a difficult period; it eliminates those who are not serious about their intention of going to the space colony. You undergo weeks of quarantine, exhaustive physical examinations, stringent decontamination, and interminable tests to make sure that you do not carry insects, bacteria, fungi, or mental problems to L5 [space station]. Only then are you permitted to board a personnel module of a heavy-lift launch vehicle which everyone refers to as the HLLV, along with 99 prospective colonists who have gone through even more rigorous tests than you have as a mere visitor.

"...During the construction phase of the colony, the staging area handled replacement supplies at the rate of 1000t a year. The growth and increasing loading of the colony required trans-shipment of an average of 50 people per week together with their personal belongings and the additional carbon, nitrogen, and hydrogen needed to sustain them in space. Oxygen, and other elements, are obtained from the Moon. Later the big demand was for lightweight, complex components fabricated for satellite solar power stations. Initially the resupply of the lunar base also came from Earth. The 150 people on the Moon require 250t of supplies and rotation of 75 people from Earth each year. Furthermore, there is traffic from the colony to Earth. Studies of past colonizations on Earth have shown that discontent with frontier life is usually such that many colonists wish to return home." The study admits, "it might be necessary to devise ways to discourage commuting."

The book describes the approach to the space station, situated in neutral gravity between the Earth and moon, and supplied from the moon base:

"The space colony appears as a giant wheel in space. Still you cannot comprehend its size, but you know it must be huge. One of the other passengers who has been on the trip before tells you it is 1800m in diameter... He points to the hub of the wheel and tells you that is where your transport is heading to dock with the space colony, explaining that local custom has named the docking area the North Pole." [emphasis added].

Might this be a code explaining the clandestine meetings of the conspirators, "beneath ice of Arctic"? My guess is that it is merely an interesting coincidence as are, in all probability, the following paragraphs from Section 4, titled "Choosing Among *Alternatives*" [emphasis added]. Again, it almost seems as if we are witnessing the mocking cant of conspirators daring us to *try* and do something about their schemes:

"Moreover, again because time was short, many of the comparisons among *alternative* subsystems were more qualitative than study group members would have liked.

"Effort devoted to *alternatives* depended upon the particular subject. A great deal of time was spent considering different forms for the habitat, how to handle the shielding and how to process lunar material. Less time was given to considering *alternative* patterns of siting the colony and its parts, of different ways to achieve life support, or of various possible transportation systems. In some cases much effort was expended but few *alternatives* were generated; an example is the system for moving large amounts of matter cheaply from the moon to the colony. No *alternative* at all was found to the manufacture of solar satellite power plants as the major commercial enterprise of the colony.

"It is important to realize that the *alternatives* described in this chapter constitute a major resource for improving the proposed design and for constructing new designs that meet other criteria. Rejection of any concept for the current baseline system does not mean that concept is fundamentally flawed. Some *alternatives* were rejected because they failed to meet the criteria, which were deliberately chosen conservatively and might well be changed on the basis of future experience or under different assumptions. Others were rejected simply because information about them was incomplete. Yet others were not chosen because their virtues were recognized too late in the study to incorporate them into a unified overall picture.

"The *alternatives* might also be useful for designing systems with other goals than permanent human settlement in space; for example, space factories with temporary crews, or laboratories. *Alternatively*, new knowledge or advances in technology, such as the advent of laser propulsion or active shielding against ionizing radiation, might make rejected subsystems very desirable." [emphases added]

Information reminiscent of the possible origin of crop circles suggested in chapter 6 of this book, "Hot Jobs and Crop Circles," is provided in subsections "Satellite Solar Power Stations: No *Alternatives*" and "Still Other *Alternatives*" [emphases added], describing the microwave transmission from space of solar-generated power, and the production of that power being a potential economic justification for space colonization.

Alternative 3 is correct in reporting that a number of astronauts had psychological difficulties after their missions in space, but that is fairly common knowledge. Comments that Buzz Aldrin made in his book *Return to Earth* particularly suggest that, as *Alternative 3* maintains, something was going on that the public wasn't being told about:

"We were to become public relations men for space exploration — in a sense, salesmen. The word made me terribly uncomfortable and self-conscious when it was first used." Speaking of his wife, Aldrin said, "I was incredulous... she had really believed all that crap that she had read about me — about her — about all of us? Suddenly all my life... became tinged with a crazy unreality."

Aldrin also described a meeting of the Lancaster, California Chamber of Commerce where he was one of the guest speakers. Roy Neal, an NBC newscaster asked Aldrin a question that Aldrin was not comfortable with: "Now that almost two years have gone by, why not tell us how it really felt to be on the moon?"

Aldrin's reaction, as described by him, was very strange. "If any one question was anathema to me, that was it. Roy, I suppose, felt he had no choice. Yet it has always been almost impossible for me to answer that question with any sort of decent response.

"My throat went dry and I became dizzy. Carefully I picked my way through a reply, thinking that all of the test pilots in the audience would burst out in laughter.

"I remember little more of the interview... I signed a few [autographs] and when the shaking became uncontrollable, I grabbed Joan and ran for the door... In the privacy of an alley near the auditorium, I choked back my emotions and quietly wept."

17

Disinfo

*T*he possibility exists that *Alternative 3* was created as "grey" dis-information, calculated to confuse and defuse the issues of elitist control, mind control, genocide, and secret space programs, by revealing yet con-cealing these truths. The purpose would be to discredit these subjects and shunt debate into conclaves of UFO True Believers, who could be counted on to hallucinate, embroider and heavily merchandise the information, thus continuing the work of the disinformers. It wouldn't be the first instance of the government (in either its overt or covert manifestation) using dis-information vectors to confuse, pacify, or stampede the populace in direc-tions of their choosing.

Along this line, Leslie Watkins' background as a writer is interesting. His books, in order of publication, are *The Sleepwalk Killers,* "a non-fic-tion study of somnambulistic violence," *The Killing of Idi-Amin,* about Watkins' experiences when imprisoned by the Amin regime, *The Unex-ploded Man,* characterized as "a thriller," although the title sounds as if it might be on the Manchurian Candidate theme, *Alternative 3, The Real Ex-orcists,* a nonfiction book about exorcism, *Private Opinions,* nonfiction about public opinion polls, *Billion Dollar Miracle,* a book about the New Zealand travel industry, and *The Story of Money,* commissioned by Bar-clays Bank.

Altogether an interesting mix of subjects, with a predominant theme that might be termed manipulative psychology. Watkins relates in a letter that during the writing of *The Killing of Idi-Amin* he was "imprisoned and threatened with death by the Amin regime in Uganda (they suspected me, falsely, of being a British spy, when I went there to cover a war for the *Daily Mail.*"

As to whether the authors of *Alternative 3* fell upon their theme through coincidence, happenstance, or enemy action, I have no idea. Watkins maintains that it was an accident, although it can be easily seen that the accident cannot have been complete. A hoax book or television show like *Alternative 3* betrays a disdain for easily-duped "commoners" only too prevalent in the attitudes of British media hacks and, especially, the upper crust owners of same.

There is much evidence to suggest that the UFO field itself, the primary forum for the discussion of *Alternative 3*, is itself largely a blind, a maze of fun house mirrors generated to twist facts, to conceal and not to reveal them. Many UFO personalities, back to the earliest days of UFO research, have had connections to military intelligence. These have been the supposed experts and opinion leaders in the field, and some have had concealed loyalties.

Todd Zechel, interviewed by Timothy Good in *Above Top Secret*, has alleged that several CIA agents infiltrated and held high positions in the early UFO organization NICAP. Zechel cites Count Nicholas de Rochefort, a member of the CIA's Psychological Warfare Staff, who was vice-Chairman of NICAP in 1956. He also names as CIA agents Bernard J. Carvalho, Chairman of NICAP's membership subcommittee, Karl Pflock, Chairman of the Washington, DC subcommittee, and G. Stuart Nixon, former assistant to NICAP's president.

Stating that Donald Keyhoe was deliberately ousted from NICAP by the CIA, Zechel says: "Maybe it's a coincidence that the founder of the CIA's Psychological Warfare Staff has been on the board [of NICAP] for nearly twenty years. Maybe it's another coincidence that Charles Lombard, a former CIA covert employee (according to himself) would seek out a retired CIA executive to run the organization (i.e. after Jack Acuff was replaced by a retired CIA agent, Alan N. Hall in 1979!)... Or maybe we're all paranoid... Perhaps Keyhoe deserved to be fired from the organization he built with his own sweat, blood, and sacrifice. The timing couldn't have been better, in any case. Keyhoe, after all, was beginning to focus on the CIA in 1969, instead of his tunnel-visioned attacks on the Air Force... if they wanted to destroy the leading anti-secrecy organization of the 1960s, they couldn't have done a better job if they'd tried."

Former CIA intelligence officer Miles Copeland, also interviewed by Timothy Good, told of a disinformation program headed by Desmond Fitzgerald of the organization's Special Affairs Staff. False press reports about UFOs were released from a number of different areas of the globe, in order to "keep the Chinese off balance and make them think we were doing things we weren't. The project got the desired results, as I remember, except that it somehow got picked up by a lot of religious nuts in Iowa and Nebraska or somewhere who took it seriously enough to add an extra chapter to their version of the New Testament!"

Ufologists William Cooper and John Lear can both be cited as having connections to the clandestine community (Cooper claiming to have been in military intelligence, Lear as a CIA operative), although they are both fond of accusing other researchers of being agents of the "Secret Government." Lear and Cooper tell essentially the same convoluted tale of U.S. government long-term collaboration with the extraterrestrial "greys," the big-headed, spindly-bodied aliens figuring prominently in current abductee tales. They maintain that the government is involved in an active process of concealing the existence of extraterrestrial invaders, a peace treaty between the aliens and the government, and the existence of collaborative alien/human bases in such places as Dulce, New Mexico. Due to the government treaty, the aliens have a degree of freedom to do their dirtywork, which apparently includes cattle mutilations, the abduction of a certain number of humans per year for use in genetic experimentation, and the implantation of humans with tiny brain control devices.

An examination of Cooper's writings frankly reveals a character which, to me, bears little resemblance to Reilly, Ace of Spies. Lear, however, has long maintained contacts in the intelligence community, and there is a framed photo in his home of Watergate spook G. Gordon Liddy, inscribed: "To John, I told em fuckin nothin."

Lear admits to having recently spent time with Gordon Novel, a man implicated in the Kennedy assassination by New Orleans District Attorney Jim Garrison and others, and alleged by his wife to have been one of the Oswald impersonators prior to the Kennedy killing. Novel himself has admitted that he was hired by Lyndon Johnson to sabotage the Garrison investigation.

Of his encounter, Lear said that Novel and another man, an "electronics expert" working for Federal Technologies Corporation, had come up with "an advanced device" for the Joint Chiefs of Staff. "During their research," Lear stated, "they had come across information the UFOs may exist, and both of them wanted to come down here and get a briefing." During the visit Novel spoke at length with Lear about UFOs and the government/alien collaboration which Lear touts.

Lear suggests: "Maybe he was sent here to disinform me. Maybe he was sent to find out how much I knew. Maybe he was sent to divert my attention from Dulce [the town near the underground New Mexico alien base Lear maintains exists, and which area is in fact a reported center for cattle mutilations in the Southwest]." Martin Cannon, writing in *UFO Uni-*

verse magazine, proposes a more likely possibility: that Novel was sent to draw attention to Lear.

Another case, that of Paul Bennewitz, is instructive. In 1979 prominent UFO field personality William Moore became interested in researcher Bennewitz' contact with a woman who had an abduction experience and maintained that she had witnessed cattle mutilations and the use of animal parts in vat experimentation. Bennewitz concluded the woman had been implanted with an alien-manufactured brain receiver and, with experience as a physicist, sought to determine the source of the electromagnetic signals he felt must be used to influence the woman.

Moore says that at the same time he was approached "by a well-placed individual within the intelligence community who claimed to be directly connected to a high-level project dealing with UFOs. This individual told me that he spoke for a small group of similar individuals who were uncomfortable with the government's continuing cover-up of the truth and indicated that he and his group would like to help me with my research into the subject in the hope and expectation that I might be able to help them find a way to change the prevailing policy and get the facts to the public without breaking any laws in the process. The man who acted as liaison between this group and myself was an Air Force Office of Special Investigations agent named Richard Doty. I knew I was being recruited, but at that point I had no idea for what."

Moore exchanged information about Bennewitz and the APRO research group he was director of for what he thought was classified information about UFOs. At the same time that Bennewitz was receiving supposed classified information, according to Moore, "Paul was gathering data from a variety of sources and amalgamating it with information being fed to him by a number of government people in whom, for some reason, he seemed to have an implicit and abiding faith. The story that emerged from this melange of fact, fiction, fantasy, hearsay, hard data and government disinformation was absolutely incredible! Yet somehow, Paul believed in it and set out on a one-man crusade to tell the world that malevolent aliens from space were in league with our government to take over the planet. What had begun in 1979 as an effort to learn whether the behavior of a woman who claimed she had been abducted by UFO aliens was being influenced by some sort of radio remote control had, in the space of less than three years, blossomed into a tale which rivaled the wildest science fiction scenario anyone could possibly imagine."

Moore says that the government's investigation of Bennewitz involved wiretaps and break-ins, and by 1982, Bennewitz had become convinced of a scenario of alien collaboration with the government, control devices, and a secret underground base at Dulce, New Mexico. This is essentially the same story circulated by John Lear, William Cooper, and others of the alien-government collaboration school.

"I know that this whole body of information is false, because I was in a position to observe much of the disinformation as it unfolded. And I can tell you that it was effective, because I watched Paul become systematically more paranoid and more emotionally unstable as he tried to assimilate what was happening to him. He had guns and knives all over his house, had installed extra locks on the doors, and he swore that 'they' (meaning the aliens) were coming through his walls at night and injecting him with hideous chemicals which would knock him out for long periods of time. He began to suffer increasing bouts of insomnia. I knew at that time that he was not far from an inevitable nervous collapse. His health had deteriorated, he had lost considerable weight, his hands shook as if from palsy, and he looked terrible. I tried to counsel him to drop the entire UFO thing before his health was completely destroyed. Not long afterward I heard he had been hospitalized and was under psychiatric care."

Summing up the experience, Moore says: "Disinformation is a strange and bizarre game. Those who play it are completely aware that an operation's success is dependent upon dropping false information upon a target or 'mark,' in such a way that the person will accept it as truth and will repeat, and even defend it to others as if it were true. One of the key factors in any successful disinformation scheme is that *it must contain some elements of truth* [emphasis added] in order to be credible. Once the information is believed, the work of counterintelligence specialists is complete. They can simply withdraw in the confidence that the dirty work of spreading their poisonous seeds will be done by others."

Other UFO cases provide clues to a manipulation that may or may not be extraterrestrial in origin. Martin Cannon in *The Controllers: A New Hypothesis of Alien Abductions* discusses the famous Betty and Barney Hill UFO abduction case as a possible case of government, not alien intervention. In 1961 the Hills were returning from a vacation trip. Passing through Groveton, New Hampshire they spotted an unusual star-like object in the night sky, and initially thought that it was a "falling star," or perhaps an airplane or satellite. Performing unusual aerial maneuvers, the "star" drew closer until they could see that it was a disk-shaped craft. The craft stopped in front of the car at a height of "eight to ten stories," and Barney Hill brought the car to a stop. The Hills were able to see humanoid figures through the windows of the saucer, and Barney Hill, afraid that he and his wife were going to be "captured," jumped back into the car and fled down the highway, leaving the UFO behind.

Within a few days Betty Hill began having nightmares about the encounter, but it was two years before the Hills sought help from Boston psychiatrist Dr. Benjamin Simon. Six months of hypnotic therapy brought out details of "missing time" and a supposed abduction aboard the saucer craft, including physical examination conducted on both of the Hills by the humanoid occupants of the UFO.

While the account of the Hills' alleged alien encounter is familiar to most individuals interested in the subject of UFOs, there are several details which are not widely-discussed, and which may point to other than the usual suppositions about contact from outer space.

The Hills' background is interesting, and perhaps made them desirable for "abduction" and mind-tampering. An interracial couple, they held prominent positions in a number of civil rights organizations (this during a time when such organizations were under surveillance and sometimes attack by the FBI and the CIA). The Hills would have been perfect subjects for the covert implantation of electronic bugs for surveillance of these organizations. Cannon points out that Barney Hill was acquainted with the head of Air Force intelligence at Pease Air Force Base, and suggests that this may have been the relationship which brought the couple to the attention of the intelligence community, not their saucer contact.

Other details of the Hills' abduction are not mentioned by Cannon, yet I believe may be significant. Betty Hill described the inhabitants of the flying saucer as wearing uniforms and billed caps ("similar to Air Force"), and speaking with a "foreign" accent. On several occasions, when Betty Hill became upset during the abduction and examination, the leader of the abductors rubbed his hand in front of her face in the familiar gesture of a hypnotist.

Barney Hill's first impression of the leader of his abductors was, "He looks like a German Nazi. He's a Nazi..." One of them, he said, was a "military pilot." During hypnosis Barney Hill said: "I thought of the Navy and the submarine, and I thought the men that moved back were just dressed in blue denims. But this other man was dressed in a black shiny coat, with a cap on."

This suggests a somewhat different event than the one portrayed on television, with standard big-headed aliens abducting and making free with the Hills. Extraterrestrials in blue denim?

Another UFO close encounter that does not seem to fit into the standard mold, is that of William "Eddie" Laxton. Researcher John Keel relates that on March 23, 1966 Laxton, an aircraft electronics instructor, was driving to Sheppard Air Force Base where he worked, approaching an intersection on Highway 70 near the Texas-Oklahoma border. A huge "fish-shaped" craft suddenly loomed in front of his car, blocking the road. Laxton estimated the object to be about 75 feet long and 8 feet deep.

Laxton said that the object "had a plastic bubble in front which was about three feet in diameter, and you could see light through it." He also remembers that the craft had numbers and letters painted vertically in black on the fuselage, either TL4768 or TL4168. Laxton noticed a man examining the craft with a flashlight, and later described him as wearing a mechanic's cap with the bill turned up — apparently a popular mode of alien dress if we take the Hill encounter into consideration.

"I got the impression due to his stooped shoulders he was about thirty to thirty-five years old. He wore either coveralls or a two-piece suit that looked like green-colored fatigues. I got the idea that he had three stripes above and three below [on his sleeve]. The above stripes were in an arch and the below stripes were in a wide V shape."

The "mechanic," on spotting Laxton, climbed a ladder and entered the craft, and the UFO soon departed. "In about five seconds," Laxton said, "it was a mile away."

Another UFO encounter linked in conclusive manner to military operations is the famous Cash-Landrum case, which took place in Dayton, Texas in 1980. Betty Cash, her friend Vickie Landrum, and Landrum's seven year old grandson were driving outside Dayton when they saw the descent of a huge UFO, flames shooting downward from the craft. The object hovered at a height of approximately 135 feet, and Cash saw it as a bright light while Landrum described a rounded top and a pointed lower portion. The car became so hot that Cash was unable to touch its outside surface.

Following the object in the car, they were surprised to see twenty-three large twin-rotor helicopters escorting it at distances no closer than three quarters of a mile. Stopping the car a number of times to observe the object, they then drove home.

It was after they had returned home that symptoms of what seemed to be radiation exposure appeared. Betty Cash's eyes swelled shut, nodules appeared on her scalp, and she suffered from nausea and vomiting. Four days after the incident she was admitted to the hospital as a burn victim. Cash had left the car to observe the object, while the other two witnesses had remained inside, and her exposure seems to have been the worst. Vickie Landrum suffered from eye inflammation and hair loss, while the child had eye inflammation and "sunburn."

Timothy Good offers clues to the nature of the object observed by Cash and Landrum, citing anonymous but, according to him, reliable sources. He says that the object has been described as an experimental nuclear powered space shuttle (just the thing to shuttle *Alternative 3* 'batch consignments' to the moon, one might say).

Cash and Landrum sued the government for their injuries, but the case was dismissed on the basis of the military's protestation that they possessed no such craft.

A strange "abduction" incident which may link to laser 'hot jobs' is related in the *SPIRAL* newsletter for April 21, 1982:

"It occurred on Dec. 11, 1979 and involved Melvin and Naomi (last name not given), a healthy couple in their early 60s. Melvin is a retired aerospace engineer 'who had received honors in the Apollo program,' according to the *MUFON UFO Journal* of March 1982. They were both at home that night, watching TV and having cheese and wine when they both simultaneously and instantly lost consciousness for no apparent reason. Afterwards they both took a 'trip' which could be described as hell. Neither could remember consciously what happened during the next two days, but after the incident both Naomi and Melvin were hospitalized — Naomi for treatment of "depressive reaction and dehydration" and Melvin for "psychotic reaction, dehydration and renal failure." Both had burns — Naomi had them on her hip and thigh, Melvin with a more serious burn on his hip which indented the bone, a burn on the top of his head, on both heels and a very severe one on his back. One of the physicians told Melvin he had "third degree high radiation burns."

"When they were finally able to recall at least parts of what happened during the two-day 'trip,' they described separate experiences of what might be considered a very bad LSD experience. The only thing is, when Naomi and Melvin were in the hospital (they were brought in reluctantly by Naomi's son) thorough examinations were given — including blood tests for possible traces of a drug, but none were found. Yet both obviously had some pretty wild hallucinations. They both remember being in a different room other than in their mobile home. Naomi felt as if she were in an "operating room" being examined, while Melvin was in a "cubicle" during the ordeal, with a girl who had "no features" and spoke in a "foreign" language. *They both heard a continuous sound like a helicopter engine* [emphasis added] during the first part of the experience. After that, their memories became distorted and they had individual bizarre experiences in their mobile home. They both thought someone or something was trying to get them. When Naomi's son came to get her, he found the furnace door was off and the thermocouple torn out despite the fact that it was below freezing that day...

"Two more pieces of the puzzle have to do with a 'black sooty film' on the TV screen, the windows of their mobile home, as well as on a macrame ornament and the drapes. They didn't find all this out until two months later when they finally returned home... To this day, none of the freakish experience has any explanation — the 'cubicle' hallucinations, the two-day blackout, the burns, the furnace, the black soot... all remains a complete mystery.

"The fact that Melvin worked on the Apollo space program would seem to tie in very neatly with the *Alternative 3* theme..."

A paragraph in the previously noted "Japanese Death Ray" document from 1945 strikes a familiar note relating to UFO contact. Describing the experiments by the Japanese to perfect an electromagnetic death ray, the document reports "Throughout this programme experiments were tried on the effectiveness of short-wave radiation in stopping engines by causing pre-ignition. It was found that the radiation was effective in this respect only when the engine was unshielded and it was sometimes necessary to tune the ignition system to the frequency by varying the length of the ignition cable." This is reminiscent of the reports of automobiles stalling in the vicinity of UFOs, opening other avenues of speculation when one thinks that some UFOs might be equipped with just this sort of electromagnetic weaponry.

Another possibly sinister note is provided by an abductee interviewed by Martin Cannon. She claimed that, while being abducted by apparent aliens, she was given a gun in a ziplock baggy. This was not a laser or a zap gun, but a standard gunpowder and bullet-firing model. The woman said her abductors told her in true Manchurian Candidate fashion: "When you see the light, you will do it tonight. Execute." The abductee also reports that, after her capture and examination, she developed urges to be around guns, feelings she had never experienced before.

Mark Chapman, the assassin of John Lennon, unpleasantly leaps to mind. Recounting the experience of the final seconds prior to shooting Lennon, Chapman said: "He walked past me and then I heard in my head said, 'Do it, do it, do it, do it,' like that. I pulled the gun out of my pocket, I handed over to my left hand, I don't remember aiming. I must have done, but I don't remember drawing the bead or whatever you call it. And I just pulled the trigger steady five times."

Chapman has been circumstantially linked with CIA assassination programs and neo-Nazi groups, and, according to a number of researchers, may have been programmed to murder Lennon. Interestingly, Chapman's family and that of George Bush's were close friends. It is also interesting to note that the same psychiatrist, Bernard Diamond, was used for the evaluation of Chapman and Sirhan Sirhan, the alleged assassin of Robert F. Kennedy.

Another woman interviewed by Martin Cannon said that during the course of being examined by the creatures who had abducted her she heard a very strange aside made by one "alien" abductor to another. "They will think it's flying saucers," the "alien" said in English.

18

To Serve Man

W hen evaluating suspected disinformation, we can proceed on the basis that the content of a cover-up or disinformation story can possibly offer an idea of what is being hidden, since in order to create an effective, self-perpetuating ruse, there must be a mix of truth and falsehood. This practice confuses and discredits past and future factual reports, linking them in the public mind with whatever incredible elements the disinformers may inject.

An analysis of current UFO stories, including those of flying saucers and the recent element of "underground alien bases," suggests that they may be cooked up to conceal actual realms of experimentation and manipulation by the government or other control factors. It is possible that UFO abductions are in fact the operation of secret mind control research, their terrestrial origins concealed through the use of advanced craft, with experimentation on unwitting subjects masked through hypnosis, RHIC-EDOM memory erasure corresponding to the familiar abductee experience of "missing time," or other means of mind control. What better way to conceal secret technology and human experimentation than to wrap the events in extraterrestrial trappings — perhaps using hallucinogens, alien masks, electronic effects, unusual craft, and even computerized "virtual reality" technology — and to keep issuing statements insisting that "alien abduction" is the product of someone's crazed imagination?

Conspiracy researcher Mae Brussell, in her radio show of 22 June, 1979 may have been the first to speculate on a possible core secret of UFO disinformation: the concealment of genetic experimentation, which may or may not be conducted in underground bases housing vats and utilizing bovine blood from cattle mutilations, and the connection of this experimentation to UFO coverup. Referring to the "aliens" encountered in UFO abduction experiences, Brussell said:

"My worst fear is, what if these people are genetically mutilated? What if they are humanoids that have been tampered with, and are being used for purpose of terror or development of outer space? What if that were happening? Or is it happening? I began to hear the description of the people in black [i.e. Men in Black] that follow up these sightings, and the physical descriptions and similarities of people that are seen — short humanoids, short arms, short necks, pointed ears, tight skin, holes for eyes — and I began to think of the psychiatrists that see the people afterwards, that hypnotize them and recount the stories, and wonder: who are the cast of characters that would be involved in the UFO situation if they're man-made? Like Mr. [Jacque] Vallee was saying, if they're not [from] outer space, if they're Nazi space scientists, if they're Nazi doctors...

"Where is Dr. Mengele? He's been working on genetics for forty years. There's a new book out about the thalidomide drug made by Merrill Richardson, given to women who were pregnant. It's interesting that pregnant women suffered from the deformities genetically, and their children were born without arms or legs — what they described as 'fins.' And I'm wondering if some of these experiments [have been performed] on these people, because that's been hushed up; we haven't seen photographs of these people since they've grown up. There were thousands of them in communities in Germany and England with the thalidomide children, and we haven't had any follow-up on that, or if it's been used since. Are we now meeting our own genetically refabricated children?"

There are in fact at least six federally-funded scientific teams working on what is termed the Human Genome Project, whose stated purpose is to map the molecular sequence of the 50,000 to 100,000 genes determining the structure and development of the human body, and whose unstated purposes may include eugenics goals. Certainly it is interesting that the center for Genome research in this country is located at Cold Springs Harbor, New York, historically the locale where eugenics research was launched.

The Genome Project has been referred to as "biology's moon shot," and, it is (no doubt under-) estimated, will take fifteen years and three billion dollars to accomplish. Salvador Luria, the scientific mentor of James Watson, discoverer of the structure of DNA, has criticized the project, saying that it is run by a "small coterie of power-seeking enthusiasts" leading us into a "kinder, gentler program to 'perfect' human individuals by 'correcting' their genomes..."

The truth may be even more sinister, and the scientists engaged in the project may or may not realize the full contents of the genetic Pandora's box they are opening. Project head James Watson, at least, has privately expressed concern about the dangers inherent in the project. At the International Conference on Recombinant DNA Molecules he whispered to a colleague (not intending that a nearby reporter should overhear), "We can't even measure the fucking risks."

Although the leadership of the Genome Project understandably emphasizes in public statements the acquisition of knowledge that may lead to the curing of disease and the elimination of genetic defects, there are many ethical questions being asked. Where will the line be drawn in restricting what those in power will decide what unborn generations should be? And will the mapping of the human genome herald a return to traditional elitist eugenics programming, unchallenged by a public with a short memory?

The Genome Project synchronizes perfectly with the social control purposes of the psychiatric and social control establishments. Until now they have had to accomplish their purposes by crude means such as drugs, electroshock, brain implants and electronic mind control, but with research into genetic determination and alteration, it may be possible to intervene prior to a person's birth. They may be able to breed out revolt, and to turn subjects into docile workers never questioning their living — or dying — conditions.

Marine Major Donald E. Keyhoe, in *Aliens from Space*, one of numerous popular UFO books he wrote trumpeting the idea of space invaders and pooh-poohing the possibility of any connection to advanced military projects, is surprisingly forthright in talking about NASA cyborg programs:

"Cyborg (cybernetic organism) is the goal of a program under NASA contract. Using chemical 'mind changers' and surgery, some future astronauts would be transformed into semi-robots... Such 'closed cycle' astronauts would be a mating of man with machine. Artificial units would replace their hearts and most other main organs. They would need no food or water — they would have built-in energy suppliers. Eventually even their brains might be replaced.

"Cyborg, the emotionless semi-robot, would be used on long journeys which could break down a normal astronaut. There is no question that it can be done — by us or an alien race."

Keyhoe quotes Dr. Toby Freedman of North American Aviation as saying, "This surgical tempering would produce a weird being who accomplishes his space mission by trading most of his physiological systems for electronic ones, whose mouth is sealed, lungs collapsed, body wastes recycled through himself, neural pathways partly severed and all his emotional feelings dissected out. He would be so fantastically changed he could never rejoin the human race."

Does the cyborg that Keyhoe and Freedman describe seem reminiscent of the "grey aliens" that so many abductees describe?

According to David Paul in *Apocalypse Culture*, "Naval Research Laboratories, the Japanese Ministry of International Trade and Industry, the U.S. Defense Advanced Research Projects Agency and other investors like Sharp and Sanyo-Denki are funding research into what is known as the Molecular Electronic Device (MED) or 'biochip.' There are several designs for these organic microprocessors, but the essential idea is to use protein molecules or synthetic organic molecules as computing elements to store information or act as switches with the application of voltage. Signal flow in this case would be by sodium or calcium ions. Others feel that artificial proteins can be constructed to carry signals by electron flow. Still another idea is to 'metalize' dead neuronal tissue to produce processing devices."

Paul quotes geneticist Kevin Ullmer, of Genex Corporation, as saying: "The ultimate scenario is to develop a complete genetic code for the computer that would function as a virus does, but instead of producing more virus, it would assemble a fully operational computer inside a cell."

Other theoretical possibilities are noted in the anonymous document "Alien and Government Secret Genetic Project Directives," which makes much of the collaboration of the U.S. government with space aliens (making it a probable candidate for disinformation, in my evaluation), but at the same time listing other possibilities I find more credible. These include researches into the production of synthetic biological organisms, experimental learning programs, and sub-race development (perhaps genetically bred for living under hostile other-planetary conditions). Other possibilities listed in the document are food-source development and functional skill specializations, by which human bodies would be altered or grown to perform certain functions, again suggesting abilities that might be desirable in a space colony.

I consider the document "Orion Based Technology, Mind Control and Other Secret Projects," which has circulated widely in the UFO community, to be highly suspect and probably another product of a government hack, although there may be some truth in it along with a disinformational spin. Regarding biological experimentation, the interviewed O.H. Krill (an alleged extraterrestrial left on Earth as an ambassador after the signing of a US/alien treaty) says:

"Human cloning was developed at the University of Utah at Salt Lake City in 1977. They first aired this on TV as part of a series. They had an alleged human clone on TV that they were interviewing. It didn't talk very well. They showed the original human and the clone. The clone was not all that successful. It took 14 months to generate a fully adult human clone in a tank. It was a two part series. The second part of the series never aired, for obvious reasons. CIA sources have confirmed that it started at the University of Utah. The government has a facility for clones. The first one was built in the Mount Hood area, about sixty miles east of Portland, Oregon. They have other facilities in other locations. Locations must have stable geomagnetic fields and other special characteristics or the cloning process does not work properly. They can replicate them faster now."

Science fiction? Quite probably, but in 1967 Cambridge physiologist Lord Rothschild, of all people, told scientists at the Weizmann Institute of Science in Israel that he considered the cloning of people would be a reality in the near future. That statement was made 25 years ago. Might cloning be a "suppressed technology" that it would be better for the public not to find out about?

The FBI keeps DNA files on those they define as "criminals," and DNA "dogtags" have now been instituted by the Army, supposedly as aid to body identification. Alan Westin of the Columbia University Department of Political Sciences has said that "there is already a dangerous call from some government individuals to extend DNA testing to broad investigative data bank collections from... the general populace."

The implementation of plans involving genetic (or even cyborg) manipulation should be made vastly easier by using a DNA "wand" that Cornell University admits to having perfected. The wand is hand-held and shoots ten million DNA-coated pellets into living flesh. There is no visible effect on the skin, and the pellets are so small that virtually no sensation is felt. This DNA wand is highly reminiscent of the reports of the hardware used on some UFO abductees by "aliens."

Stories of human vat experimentation and the frequent observation of unmarked or military helicopters in the vicinity of cattle mutilations provide a suggestion that the military or some other organization are doing experimentation requiring large quantities of blood for its accomplishment.

In the classic mutilation scenario the cow appears to have been completely drained of blood, while still living, in some unknown quick procedure. Using advanced surgical techniques, blood and organs are removed; usually one ear, one eye, the tongue and the anus. The animal is left behind, often in a highly unnatural position: flat on its back with legs sticking into the air, with no blood in the carcass or on the ground around it, and no foot or hoofprints surrounding it, not even those of the dead animal. Many of the carcasses also appear to have been dropped from a height, as if from a hovering aircraft.

The first official reports of mutilated livestock came from Colorado in the early 1960s where, in two counties, there were combined reports of 169 mutilated cows. Since that time the mutilation of more than 70,000 head of cattle, horses and other domestic and wild animals has been reported across the U.S. as well as in Canada, England, Brazil and even Kenya. Yet there has not been a single arrest, nor a single perpetrator caught in the act. Certainly, if there had been 70,000 cars or televisions stolen there would have been arrests and people doing jail time.

One possible clue to cattle mutilation is that the removing of the cow's blood may be the prime focus of the operation, this because of the similarity of bovine and human blood. *Insight* magazine for September 18, 1989 announced that a supplement to human blood made from cow's blood was about to be clinically tested. The magazine related that scientists were working on a blood supplement called Hemopure I, and that it could be used in short term situations, such as emergency replacement of blood lost through car accidents and shootings. Cow hemoglobin, it was reported, is similar in its amino acid and oxygen content to human hemoglobin, contains 40 times more red blood cells than an equal amount of human blood, and can be stored indefinitely.

There are additional clues that are not often mentioned in the popular media. Many "mutes" have been found to have been marked with fluorescent paint, probably as an aid to identification in the dark. A large percentage of mutilated cattle have also been found to have been injected with strains of harmful Clostridium bacteria (of which blackleg and malignant adema are members of the genus). In an investigation of bacteriological warfare in 1970, Senator Frank Church's Senate Select Committee on Intelligence determined that the CIA had stockpiled canisters of this same bacteria.

One persistent rumor has been that cattle are used in biological testing due to the similarity of the membrane of the eye with that of a certain ethnic group. Researcher Ed Sanders interviewed G.C. Errianne, a former member of an unspecified intelligence agency, who admitted that secret bacterial research was being conducted in the United States and that these researches were targeted "in regard to Oriental warfare." Sanders also interviewed reporter Bill Hendrix of KTVX-TV in Salt Lake City, who confirmed that Dugway Proving Ground in Utah had done research on a specifically anti-Oriental biological weapon.

The anonymous COM-12 intelligence briefing provides another link between government testing and UFO disinformation. Citing the Wackenhut organization as being in charge of a number of covert operations around the world, the COM-12 document places the group under the umbrella of a secret government project termed "Yellow Lodge":

"The 'Yellow Lodge' project involves the infiltration and covert operations of advanced chemical, biological and, in some cases, weapons development. These activities, due to the sovereign status of Indian lands [where they are conducted], can be carried out by private and covert operations without answering to the legitimate arm of the U.S. government. This scenario is especially true of the Jicarilla Apache lands, as well as many other reservations in the American Southwest — the largest of these being the umbra-classification base known as D6 (Dulce) in the state of New Mexico."

It is interesting to note that the alleged underground base at Dulce figures as the most popular locale for government-alien collaboration in the writings of the extraterrestrial invasion school of UFO writing, as, for instance, in the probable hoax Dulce File.

There has been a good deal of speculation about the cattle mutilations being performed by Satanists or other occultists during ritual activity, but it is extremely odd that none of the perpetrators have been caught in the act, or arrested later. A possibility exists that these crimes are being committed by someone above the law. As to whether it is the government using unmarked helicopters, Satanists, or aliens in their UFOs, I think the first possibility most likely.

There have been other mutilations that the media are not telling you about. A media blackout has been enforced on the subject of traffic in human organs, sold almost entirely to the wealthy, and the farming of these organs in Central America.

In the article "Loathsome Sale of Human Flesh" in the virtually underground Athens, Georgia *Observer,* researcher Joe Ionno states:

"According to a Resolution of the European Parliament on the Trafficking of Central American Children, 'human farms' complete with 'fattening houses' have been discovered in Honduras and Guatamala.

"In San Pedro Sula, Honduras, it was reported that near one such farm, corpses of infants were discovered that 'had been stripped of a number of organs.'

"In Guatamala, at another 'human farm' babies ranging from 11 days old to four months old were discovered. They 'were sold to wealthy American or Israeli families whose children needed organ transplants at the cost of $75,000 per child,' according to the director of the farm who made this claim during his arrest.

"Though extremely reputable newspapers such as *Le Monde* (France), the *Guardian* (England) and the Honduran journal *El Tiempo* have carried stories of such atrocities, none, to my knowledge, have appeared in any major U.S. publications...

"The July 22, 1990 issue of *La Prensa Dominical* (Honduras)... reported that police in El Salvador had uncovered a smuggling ring headed by (what else?) a lawyer which was buying children for resale in the U.S., noting that 20,000 children disappear every year in Mexico.

"The report states, 'The most gory fact, however, is that many little ones are used for transplant or organs to children in the United States,' and further suggests that this may be the reason that the highest rate of kidnapping of children from infants to 18 year olds is in those regions of Mexico which border on the U.S.

"*El Tiempo* reports that an appeals court judge in Honduras ordered 'a meticulous investigation into the sale of Honduran children for the purpose of using their organs for transplant operations.'

"The Honduran Secretary of the National Council of Social Services (the agency in charge of adoptions) reported that children 'were being sold to the body traffic industry' for organ transplants.

Ionno quotes as sources *Le Monde,* September 21, 1988; the *Guardian Weekly,* October 2, 1990; *El Tiempo,* August 10, August 17 and September 21, 1988, and Noam Chomsky's book *Deterring Democracy.*

A question arises. When genes can be tinkered with and, as is the case now, copyrighted, when biological forms can be altered and meshed, dissected with ease and without the slightest compunction, where will the line be drawn between humans and veal cutlets? Will the "lower classes" then no longer be the "useless eaters," as they were termed by the Nazis and by former CIA director William Colby, but the "useful eaten"?

I am reminded of the classic Twilight Zone episode in which 'friendly' aliens come to Earth to invite humans to return with them to see their world. Human reporters acquire a book written by the aliens entitled *To Serve Man.* As the hero of the tale is stepping into the aliens' saucer his secretary rushes up with the news that they have translated the book — and that it is a gourmet cookbook.

I received an unexpected and startling reality check after writing the above in an unattributed magazine clipping reprinted in Michael A. Hoffman's *Secret Societies and Psychological Warfare.* Titled "Eating Raoul... and Others," the article wonders, "How would you like to bite into a part-human bacon cheeseburger?" asks Michael Colgan, Ph.D., in the journal *Nutrition and Fitness* (Vol. 10, No. 1 & 2). In five years they'll be at a burger stand near you, predicts the author. The U.S. Department of Agriculture's research center in Beltsville, Md., has been inserting human genes into fertilized swine eggs, and a herd of "hupigs" now resides at the center. One goal of such research is to manufacture "spare parts for humans," that is, genetically engineered organs to replace diseased human organs; another goal is to "design" animals for more efficient meat production.

"The USDA creatures reportedly suffer from coordination so poor that they can barely walk. They also are subject to arthritis and lung and gut diseases. State and federal laws severely restrict access by journalists and the public, and photographs of the 'hunimals' are forbidden."

Pondering the possible motives of government and para-government genetic and cyborg projects, I can see that ultimately they may be intended to violate and destroy the last barrier to world totalitarian control: humanness itself.

Gone, long gone, is the consideration of human life as having an inherent personality and value. These "imaginative" scientists in the employ of super-capitalists seem to have lost sight of everything but the power inherent in their vision ("Power is the great aphrodisiac," so sayeth Henry Kissinger). They may see life as raw material and the ultimate energy-utilization extension, as a remote control web for augmenting control intention. Life, intelligence, may be viewed by them as a malleable, virtually unlimited sub-control mechanism that can be linked, even atomically, with such technologies as molecular robotics and nanotech (ie. molecular manufacturing, controlling the structure of matter) to mold universe energies into instantaneously-crystallized realities, Xanadus for the gratification of these would-be immortals. Beyond mind control, this would be tantamount to "soul control."

Is life viewed by these "scientists" and their bosses as slave-energy that can be shaped and replicated at will, formed into "bodies" and "body-corporations" of protoplasm, as submissive genii for manifesting the whims of the elite?

19

Other Alternatives

*A*lternatives 1 and 2, according to the book, were also considered as possible solutions for the deteriorating conditions on Earth. These consisted of, respectively, a plan to atomically blow holes in the atmosphere to release pollution into space, and a plan to create subterranean dwellings for the world's elite to escape to when things on the surface get too bad.

There was, in fact, a program of upper atmosphere detonation of nuclear weapons that took place in the fifties and sixties. According to *The Leading Edge* magazine, in the article "Project Argus and the Rainbow Bombs: United States Nuclear Detonations in Space":

"Around 1958, the significant implications of the Earth's magnetic fields and radiation belts for future military activities were what drew the attention of government physicists. Nicholas Christofilos, a physicist working at the University of California's Livermore Radiation laboratory, developed techniques to harness and control the energy released in hydrogen fusion reactions. Christofilos used magnetic confinement fields. When the Soviets launched Sputnik I, Christofilos decided that the Earth's magnetic field could be used to contain an artificial band of relativistic electrons. He speculated that this artificial radiation belt could be made intense enough to destroy satellites in orbit. The belt would produce worldwide radio noise on the HF and VHF radio bands that carried the bulk of military communications. By accurately calculating the site for an explosion of a nuclear device, its effects could be made to occur over a specific target area. Christofilos urged that the government test his postulates by exploding a nuclear device in space. Christofilos' superiors at Livermore placed his papers under top security control and advised the President's Science Advisory group of the matter. The resulting program became Project Argus."

Project Argus tests took place, the anonymous article states, in the South Atlantic, August 27, 1958, with a one kiloton bomb exploded at two hundred kilometer altitude; in the South Atlantic on August 30, 1958, a one kiloton bomb exploded at 250 kilometer altitude; and in the South Atlantic on September 6, 1958, a one kiloton bomb exploded at an altitude of 500 kilometers. Post Argus testing included a 1.4 megaton bomb launched from Johnston Island on July 9, 1962 and exploded at an altitude of 400 kilometers. Along with the American testing, there have been several Soviet nuclear explosions in space. All were launched from Siberia and included the October 22, 1962 launch of a 200 kiloton bomb; the October 28, 1962 launch of an 800 kiloton weapon; and the November 1, 1962 launch of a 1 plus megaton weapon.

The result of all this "testing" has been quite different from the proposed solution of Alternative 1, to wit: the tests created two intense belts of radiation around the Earth. These radiation belts have, at the very least, cost the space programs of all nations billions of dollars. The only effective radiation shielding from these radiation belts is lead, and as it is too heavy to be used, this has forced craft with cargos sensitive to radiation (like living things) to be launched in steeper and vastly more expensive trajectories than would have been needed in order to get through the Van Allen belts. The dubious scientific triumph of upper atmosphere testing was decried by some scientists at the time, but their protests have long since been forgotten.

In what may be only coincidence with the Alternative 2 proposals, as reported in "The Effects of Atomic Weapons" from the Los Alamos laboratory, as early as September, 1950 the Defense Department had its eyes on underground base construction, calling such construction "desirable," and reporting that "There are apparently no fundamental difficulties in constructing and operating underground various types of important facilities."

In the proceedings of the Second Protective Construction Symposium on Deep Underground Construction in 1959, sponsored by the U.S. Air Force and carried out by the Rand Corporation think tank (a CIA-funded group that have plunged their thumbs deep into many a secretive pie-graph), it was stated,

"We have just prepared cost estimates on using a continuous shaft-sinking device for a contractor bidding on an Air Force Titan installation in Colorado. This one machine would bore tunnels varying in diameter from 10 ft. to 45 ft. Just as airplanes, ships and automobiles have given man mastery of the surface of the Earth, tunnel-boring machines and shaft-sinkers will give him access to the subterranean world. It is our aim to provide

machines which will supply the ever-increasing demand in mind and construction of underground facilities."

The RAND Corporation also investigated the use of atomic bombs to
blast underground cavities for habitation.

Russell Miller, of the Colorado School of Mines, and director of the
Center for Space Mining in Boulder, Colorado, has worked on studies for
underground cities on the moon and Mars. One method which has been
proposed by him for the building of underground extraterrestrial colonies
would be to use missiles to drive holes fifty feet beneath the Lunar or
Martian soil, and then to use atomic bombs to blast out huge cavities. Ig-
loos would be constructed over the holes, and plastic bags would be inserted into the cavities and then inflated. Workers could then construct liv-
able habitats underground.

In the late 1970s it was revealed that an underground city in Bluemont,
Virginia, dubbed "Mount Weather," was operated by the previously discussed government agency FEMA and staffed with one thousand mostly
civilian workers. Mount Weather is part of FEMA's COG (Continuity of
Government) plans, providing for the escape of the President and four
thousand other government officials in event of unstipulated catastrophe;
nuclear, revolutionary, or otherwise. Built at a cost of over one billion dollars and costing $42 million per year to operate, Mount Weather is a city of
offices which includes a dining hall, sleeping quarters, and situation rooms
with electronic map displays for the proper *Dr. Strangelove* ambiance.

Another facility, the Alternate National Military Command, also known
as Raven Rock or Site R, is located five miles north of Camp David, under
650 feet of granite. Known as the "Underground Pentagon," the 265,000
square foot bunker was built in 1949 on the orders of Harry Truman, and
has a staff of 350.

Up to fifty other underground military installations are located in the
United States, and are funded by huge "black budget" allocations. Tim
Weiner, Pulitzer prize-winning author of *Blank Check*, has stated that more
black budget money goes into these underground projects than into any
other kind of project. This gives rise to the speculation that the "current
crop of disinformation," as William Moore puts it, about government collaboration with evil aliens in underground bases, is very likely aimed to
confuse the purposes of underground facilities in the public mind.

There is a possibility that some of these underground facilities are utilized for the purposes Louis Jolyon West suggested for a converted Nike
base in California in the 1960s: populace control by the implantation of
brain control devices. These electronic brain implants do exist (and have
been shown in x-rays of both abductees and mental patients), and it may be

significant that in alien abduction stories the devices are often said to be inserted in precisely the same way that psycho-surgeons implant them: nasally. Indeed, the activities of "aliens" described by "UFO abductees" are strikingly reminiscent of the programming operations that the CIA and other organizations have been shown to perform — at least sometimes without the benefit of flying saucers.

The bases may serve other purposes, including COG (as it is termed), and what is essentially an infrastructure for conducting secret military research projects. What is not often mentioned in discussions of the purposes of the underground bases is that one of the threats that they are meant to protect against is an uprising by the American people. From the safety of the underground installations the current American dictator can hole-up with his military and exterminate any possible threat from above ground.

I consider it highly unlikely that the underground bases have anything to do with outer space aliens (I don't reject the possibility out of hand, it is just that I have seen no plausible evidence substantiating a government-alien collaboration, and much evidence to suggest that this story is cooked up by and serves the government by confusing the issue).

Researcher Michael Lindemann, in a lecture given in San Diego in 1991, talked about his beliefs about the underground bases:

"There is indeed another government operating, and that government... operates primarily behind the scenes. Other researchers have called it 'The Secret Government' and others have called it 'The High Cabal,' and it is a group of people, a very elite group of non-elected, self-appointed people who guide the evolution of policy from behind the scene. These are people who transcend partisan politics, indeed who transcend the rule of law, with no thought whatsoever for the dictates of the Constitution. These are people who regard themselves as the only true guardians and crafters of geopolitical reality, and they regard us, indeed they regard our elected officials, as mere mortals. These people are the self-appointed Olympians. They have done many things in the name of an agenda which is their own, which we would consider appalling and reprehensible. Indeed, these things are criminal, but they are more than criminal, because they have sapped and usurped the rights and privileges and possibilities for our future. These people are running a kind of 'Endgame' right now. They are trying to determine how they will survive the End Time. Whether that End Time comes as a kind of Biblical Apocalypse, or more likely comes as the catastrophic collapse of the environment, coupled with the catastrophic population bomb, and all the other things that may indeed 'get our goat,' whether it comes as the collapse of the banking system which looks to be only days away, or the collapse of the world economy, there are many things that could get us, and these people, in effect, are building their own version of Noah's ark. And that Noah's ark they are building is underground: underground bases, indeed all over the world, but particularly in the United States. Huge underground bases which actually festoon the underground geography of our continent in a way that would probably stun and shock you. ...These are places that are capable of supporting on an on-going basis some tens of thousands of people, so across the country it may be possible to save an elect remnant of some hundreds of thousands of people who will be the cream of the civilization that is meant to survive the Apocalypse, or the downfall, or... whatever it is that is out there getting us. Mere mortals will have to fend for themselves."

Better, the nation's clandestine agencies seem to think, that we should believe that Earth has been invaded by murderous grey aliens in disk craft than realize that preparations are being made for the total, rather than partial suspension of the Constitution and the inauguration of an American dictatorship, possibly in the configuration of the much-touted New World Order.

An instructive study funded by the Trilateral Commission (a highly influential global organization whose origin can be traced back to the Rockefellers and the Rhodes' Round Table) is titled *The Crisis of Democracy: Report on the Governability of Democracies to the Trilateral Commission.* The paper was authored by Samuel Huntington in 1975 and provides insight into attitudes of the international controllers and goals guiding the government.

The study diagnoses the problems of the world as stemming, since "the democratic surge of the 1960s," from too much "democracy," and that "arenas where democratic procedures are appropriate are limited." Prescribed for this malady is a strengthening of elitist control, including the lowering of expectations among the poor and middle class, and a marshalling of power in the executive branch of U.S. government.

"The trend of the last decade toward the steady diminution of the power of the President should be stopped and reversed," the study states. "The President clearly has the responsibility for insuring national action on critical matters of economic and foreign policy. He cannot discharge that responsibility if he is fettered by a chain of picayune legislative restrictions and prohibitions."

The study proposes further linkages of government and business in economic planning, the pacification of labor, and increased press "self-regulation," i.e. self-censorship ("But there is also the need to assure to the government the right and the ability to withhold information at the source.") Also mentioned in the study is the need for education to be geared to "the constructive discharge of the responsibilities of citizenship," and that "a program is necessary to lower the job expectations of those who receive a college education."

Lest you think I exaggerate... Huntington feels that many of the problems facing our society are due to too much participation by the populace, since a functional system requires "some measure of apathy and noninvolvement." He goes on to say, "Previously passive or unorganized groups in the population, blacks, Indians, Chicanos, white ethnic groups, students, and women now embarked on concerted efforts to establish their claims to opportunities, positions, rewards, and privileges, which they had not considered themselves entitled [sic] before... Some of the problems of governance in the United States today stem from an excess of democracy... Needed, instead, is a greater degree of moderation in democracy... For a quarter-century the United States was the hegemonic power in a system of world order. The manifestations of the *democratic distemper*, [emphasis added] however have already stimulated uncertainty among allies..."

Confirming dictatorial plans of our leaders, elected and otherwise, are other statements about the planned New World Order. The CFR's Zbigniew Brzezinski in his book *Between Two Ages: America's Role in the Technetronic Era* gave a particularly explicit rendering. Brzezinski, a major theorist in One World circles, postulates a multiple stage evolution in man's history, beginning with a poverty-ridden 'religious' existence evolving into nationalism. The next stage, according to Zbig, is Marxism, leading into a final 'Technetronic' era. In the Technetronic era "the nation state as a fundamental unit of man's organized life has ceased to be the principal creative force: International banks and multinational corporations are acting and planning in terms that are far in advance of the political concepts of the nation-state." Reassuring vision, what?

An article which contains a kind of "Alternative 4" is the Byzantine "Franciscan Document," sent anonymously to me in 1991, and published in my anthology *Secret and Suppressed*. It purports to be a synthesis of secret information discovered in the Vatican Library by an unnamed Franciscan monk, and the inked imprint of a Vatican library entry chit at the end of the document lends it a degree of credibility. The document goes into an extensive revisionist history of the Roman Catholic Church, the Western world, and the actions of secret elitist cliques in controlling and disposing of humanity in properly sinister ways. The section that may relate to Alternative 4 follows:

"Current policies of the elite regarding the general estate of the commoners, as I myself have seen and read, is telling. While a policy of division, factionalism and antagonism is the order of the day (particularly in the United States, where what must be the most diversified population on Earth is kept in a state of turmoil by divisive legislation intended to provoke interracial strife and social stratification), there are two primary schools of thought regarding the actual use to which the subjects are to be put. While there is general agreement across the board with the notion that the commoners must be downbred, in order to reduce their intelligence and make them less apt to rise up in rebellion, a large faction - who appear to be holding sway - counsel a massive slaughter of the majority of the 'useless eaters.' ...The plan appears to be to reduce the world population overall to more manageable numbers; these survivors may then be limited as to reproduction, numbers maintained at just the level necessary to insure a force of slaves. The reason behind this reduction is among the most frightening revelations I feel I shall make: according to the best estimates of clique-employed climatologists, the world - contrary to the current 'Greenhouse Effect' story - is drawing inexorably toward another glaciation. The 'Ice Ages' are always spoken of in the past tense, always treated as occurances in prehistory, never to be repeated; however, glaciation has been the norm for this world since roughly two million years ago; alternating cycles of glaciation and warm interstadial, following an approximate one-hundred-thousand year cycle (ninety thousand years of glaciation, followed by ten thousand of interstadial, plus or minus as much as two thousand years) are the normal climate of our Earth, since the end of the Pliocene era (or perhaps slightly earlier). When the icesheets once again advance, it is the plan of the elite to move the trappings of civilization south, a forced march of laden slaves to the southern hemisphere (the glaciers cover only the northern climes), and to this end, 'housecleaning' has already begun. AIDS ravages primarily (though not exclusively) third-world populations, hence the southern lands will be defenseless; massive tracts are already being cleared and prepared for construction in South America and North America - expected to be covered, by the middle of the twenty-second century, with a two-mile thick blanket of ice - is being treated as a garbage bin, industrial effluvia of the most noxious varieties being poured out all over the land; it will cease to be of use to the elite, ergo it must be rendered useless to anyone else. Even the most dangerous of the industrial wastes will break down and be reassimilated by the soil in ninety thousand years, hence when the ice clears, a trek back to the north will be possible, if desired. In the interim, the commoners are kept palliated, entertained, too busy to investigate the world around them - and reduced, by slow attrition of incurable disease, to a desired size."

It is true that, until the middle 70s, the popular and scientific press did not talk about global warming but instead about a looming Ice Age. During the International Geophysical Year of 1958-59 scientists took thousands of core samples of Antarctic and Greenland ice, and throughout the sixties paleoclimatologists attempted to construct a history of this planet's prehistoric weather. The scientists concluded that Ice Ages occurred with far greater frequency than had previously been thought, and that we are now well into a pre-glacial cooling trend. Current warmer weather was explained by positing cycles within cycles in weather patterns, and that while the overall trend was toward an inevitable Ice Age, with perhaps 2,000 to 6,000 years to reach full glaciation, there would be recurrent periods of brief warming.

The CIA got in on the action with the August 1974 report, "A Study of Climatological Research as it Pertains to Intelligence Problems," providing a survey of then-current research, all of it seeming to say that an Ice Age was in fact due. The document lists "significant" research projects (including one being conducted by the RAND Corporation), and concludes:

"Leaders in climatology and economics are in agreement that a climatic change is taking place and that it has already caused major economic problems throughout the world. As it becomes more apparent to the nations around the world that the current trend is indeed a long-term reality, new alignments will be made among nations to insure a secure supply of food resources. Assessing the impact of climatic change on major nations will, in the future, occupy a major portion of the Intelligence Community's assets." Really?

"It is increasingly evident," the study continues, "that the Intelligence Community must understand the magnitude of international threats which occurs as a function of climatic change. These methodologies are necessary to forewarn us of the economic and political collapse of nations caused by a worldwide failure in food production. In addition, methodologies are also necessary to project and assess a nation's propensity to initiate militarily large-scale migrations of their people as has been the case for the last 4,000 years."

Another CIA study released in the same year, "Potential Implications of Trends in World Population, Food Production and Climate," indicates that, "In the worst case if climate change caused grave shortages of food despite U.S. exports, the potential risks to the U.S. would also rise. There would be increasingly desperate attempts on the part of powerful but hungry nations to get grain any way they could. *Massive migrations, sometimes backed by force*, [emphasis added] would become a live issue and political and economic instability would be widespread. In the poor and powerless areas, population would have to drop to levels that could be supported. The population 'problem' would have solved itself in the most unpleasant fashion."

So how did the current Greenhouse scenarios evolve? Although the evidence that we are experiencing global warming is persuasive, there is a possibility that this might comprise a glitch within a longer overall tendency toward another Ice Age, in support of the "Franciscan Document" and the CIA studies. It is not impossible, even, that studies of glacial cooling have been suppressed since the 1980s, or even the mid-70s, when *Alternative 3* appeared. Why?

Humans have never been very good at taking action in advance of disaster, and 'closing the barn door after the horse escapes' fairly well summarizes the populace's handling of problems, or so it seems to me. If an impending Ice Age is thousands of years ahead of us, why bother doing anything now? On the other hand, if global warming and the Greenhouse Effect could kill us all in the next thirty years, it should be obvious that we had better do something, and pretty damned fast.

With global warming we have a clear warning that, given enough propagandizing, might even be heeded. It has been widely professed that it will take an international effort to alleviate the Greenhouse Effect, requiring that the peoples of Earth drastically alter their lifestyles toward austerity (as foreshadowed by the propaganda of the Carter administration), which in addition will require some sort of planetary governing organization and police force to ensure compliance to its edicts. Global warming, factual or not, is tailor-made to the creation of a One World Government, and it seems likely that if there was no Greenhouse Effect it would be in the One Worlders' best interests to create one.

20

Das Marsprojekt

*O*ne of the difficulties in researching *Alternative 3* was that the evidence kept leading me in a direction that I wasn't particularly happy to go in: toward the Nazis. Again and again the Nazi connections kept cropping up in association with *Alternative 3* themes, but it was a connection which for obvious reasons I was reluctant to make.

Frankly, the Nazis are 'old hat,' almost a joke amongst the politically correct of today. I was reluctant to raise the specter of latter-day Nazism for fear of a dismissal as off-handed as my own reactions to *Alternative 3* on first reading. And yet, in researching the shape of totalitarian control during this century I saw that the plans of the Nazis manifestly did not die with the German loss of World War II. The ideology and many of the principal players survived and flourished after the war, and have had a profound impact on postwar history, and on events taking place today.

A possibility, which I admit is wild speculation, yet at the same time comprises a startling alignment of facts, is that *Alternative 3* is an expression of Nazi occult doctrine and that there is a long term elitist program to abandon Earth and to implement another step in Hitler's "Final Solution."

Adolf Hitler's occult orientation apparently began when, at ten years of age, he attended the Lambach Abbey School in Lambach am Traum, Austria. The abbot of the school was steeped in metaphysical doctrine, including astrology and 13th century Catharism, which had much in common with the Templar-styled occultism that Hitler would later delve into. Upon return from his travels in the East where he had engaged in Sufi studies, the abbot directed that a swastika be engraved over the entrance to the abbey, in addition to having them engraved on all the religious icons of the school and in the four corners of the building. Obviously, there was something about the power of the swastika that impressed him.

It was at Lambach Abbey that Hitler met Benedictine monk Adolf Joseph Lanz, who was later to introduce him to Vienna's occultist-racialist orders. Lanz, after doffing his monk's habit, formed the Order of the New Temple in 1905, and was the publisher of the Order's *Ostara* magazine. *Ostara's* emblem was the swastika, and the organization promoted Aryan Templarism and a war with worldwide Jewry, who were seen to be the secret masters behind the manipulation of world political and financial systems. Qualifications for joining the New Templars included having blonde hair and blue eyes, slender hands and feet, and an elongated cranium. Lanz also proposed that there should be colonies of New Templars founded away from what he saw to be the negative influence of towns and cities, and he compiled a handbook for those wishing to be future colonists.

While Hitler maintained that his National Socialism began when he joined the German Workers' Party and found a young political group with whose principals he could identify, this explanation ignores the group's existence as a front for the occultist, espionage and assassination network of the Thule Society, of which Hitler held membership as a "Visiting Brother." Freemasonic-inspired and associated with the Vril Society, the origin of both groups can be traced through English occult Fascist influences to the writings of Edward Bulwer-Lytton, author of *Vril: The Power of the Coming Race,* the godfather of the British Round Table group.

Thule and Vril proposed the extermination of "inferior" races and the creation of an Aryan race of supermen, in what was essentially a radical eugenic outlook. Thule was led by Baron von Sebottendorf, an expert in Sufism and Eastern affairs, astrologer and occultist, and it was in this group that Hitler met Karl Haushofer, reportedly the author of the geopolitical section of *Mein Kampf,* the manuscript of which is said to have been passed by Rudolf Hess to Hitler while he was imprisoned in Landsberg Fortress after the Munich *putsch.* Haushofer was an expert in Oriental and Sufi mysticism and a leading member of Vril, in close contact with British Viceroy Lord Kitchener, the Isis-Urania Temple of Hermetic Students of the Golden Dawn, as well other English mystics and mystical groups. Haushofer believed in a philosophy of "blood and soil"; that a race's survival depends upon *lebensraum* (translation: living space, incidentally the title of the Johnny Dolphin poem referred to in the chapter on Biosphere II), and that a vital race, to remain so, must continually expand and conquer "inferior races." He is reported to have said to a group of students which included Rudolf Hess that, "Space is not only the vehicle of power; it is power."

Hitler seems to have seen himself as, among other things, a latter-day leader of the historic Teutonic Knights, whose history includes their origin as kindred to the mysterious Knights Templar. The Teutonic Knights clad themselves in the familiar white mantle of the Templars, which was emblazoned with a black, rather than a red Eastern cross, and were the historical possessors of the Ordenstaat or Ordensland principality, a territory extending from Prussia and including Finland and portions of Russia. Their legendry identifies them as the guardians of the Holy Grail, the magical cup reputed to have held Jesus' blood or, in an alternate version, an engraved tablet of stone which contained the secrets of ancient Aryan magic.

Hitler may have best explained his beliefs about the Grail when he stated: "We shall form an Order, the Brotherhood of the Templars, around this Holy Grail of the pure blood." Is it possible that Hitler saw through the metaphorical-initiatory nature of the Jesus Christ legend, and believed this cup of blood to be an ancient metaphor (and perhaps simultaneously an historic, even magical physical relic) symbolizing Aryan racial purity?

Another influence on the Hitlerian occult cosmology was *Wel* (for *Welteislehre*, "the doctrine of eternal ice"), first expressed in the book *Glazialkosmogonie* (1912) by Hans Horbiger, a man whom Hitler met on several occasions and whom he is said to have equated in importance with Copernicus. It occurs to me that Wel may have been the inspiration for Immanuel Velikovsky's famous *Worlds in Collision*, although Velikovsky understandably didn't go out of his way to emphasize this connection.

Wel supposes that the nature of the universe is an eternal attraction-repulsion between cosmic ice and fire, and that this principle governs everything, including man's destiny. Star systems in the cosmos of *Wel* were caused by blocks of cosmic ice plunging into stars, creating vast explosions. Horbiger believed the history of the Earth to be one of successive cataclysms and the resultant rise and fall of races of giants, demi-gods, and other mutations, a concept echoing Aryan mythology and Thule doctrine. He also maintained that the moon was the third satellite that the Earth had captured, 12,000 years in the past, and that one of the laws of eternal ice was that the planets are subject to a continual spiralling motion into the maw of the central Sun (a possible symbolism of the swastika?). Horbiger predicted that another Earthly cataclysm was inevitable. He believed that as the moon approached the Earth it would explode due to gravitational forces, and that this would probably destroy all life on the planet.

In *Hitler Speaks*, Hitler is quoted as having said to Danzig Mayor Rauschning: "Just as, at the dawning of a new geological era, the whole world collapses in a gigantic crack, new mountains rise up while gaping abysses open up, and new plains and seas take shape, so will the present structure of Europe be capsized in an immense cataclysm... The only chance for Germany to resist this pressure will be to seize the initiative and take control of the inevitable upheaval from which will come a new dawning of history."

Since Hitler did believe Horbiger's cosmological theories, then his Thule-inspired racialist philosophy might have compelled him to look far afield for a new Fatherland, away from the doomed Earth. He may also have seen the non-Aryan "sub-human" races as the labor necessary to achieve this cosmic destiny, minions of army ants laboring in underground factories in the construction of the ultimate V-2.

Hitler revealed his greater ambitions when he said, "I had to encourage 'national' feelings for reasons of expediency; but I was already aware that the 'nation' idea could only have a temporary value. The day will come when even here in Germany what is known as 'nationalism' will practically have ceased to exist. What will take its place in the world will be a universal society of masters and overlords." In retrospect, this is a particularly modern vision.

Again in *Hitler Speaks,* Hitler is quoted as having said that humanity was evolving into two types, a new age man and a class of undermen. "I might call the two varieties the god-man and the mass animal... Man is becoming God — that is the simple fact. Man is God in the making."

Hitler, interestingly enough, had his own "alternatives," numbering four, which are outlined in *Mein Kampf* (the title a kind of pun, mirroring the Darwinian emphasis on evolutionary "struggle"). Like *Alternative 3,* Hitler foresaw a coming world of scarcity, and emphasized that there were limits to the "carrying capacity" of German resources. He proposed four possible solutions.

The first would be birth control for the Germans, to achieve population growth limits that could be sustained.

The second solution would be the use of modern technologies to increase resource yield in the Fatherland. Hitler pointed to the underlying problems with both of these options, arguing that a people whose numbers remained the same while living in an inevitably shrinking environment or natural resource base would eventually have to deal with "culturally inferior but more brutal and more natural peoples."

Hitler's third option was German interdependence with other nations. This he rejected because of the need to entrust the survival of the Aryan race to the whims of other nation states and their puppet masters.

The fourth option was war. Hitler summed up this option by saying, "We must, therefore, cooly and objectively adopt the standpoint that it is certainly not the intention of Heaven to give one people fifty times as much land and soil in this world as another... we must not let political boundaries obscure the boundaries of eternal justice... The law of self-preservation goes into effect."

In summation Hitler said that, "The folkish philosophy finds the importance of mankind in its basic racial elements. In the state it sees on principle only a means to an end and it construes its end as the preservation of the racial existence of man... And so the folkish philosophy of life corresponds to the innermost will of nature, since it restores the free play of forces which must lead to a continuous mutual higher breeding, until at last the best of humanity, having achieved possession of this Earth, will have a free path for activity *in domains which will lie partly above it and partly outside it.*" [emphasis added]

Relating to what may have been Hitler's cosmic ambitions, American educator John Taylor Gatto has commented upon the unexamined agenda of a West based upon what he sees as a European hereditary elite of primarily Aryan descent. Gatto states in "The Dying American Family and the Viking Mind" that, "Institutions would be created — adoption — compulsion-schools — vast hierarchical corporations — gigantic standing armies and navies — a government comprising 10% of the total population! — these and more would turn American social life into a scientific hive, a place where everybody's values, clothing, eating habits would be reflections of the clean mechanical style of a Viking elite... Upon the success of this plan depended salvation of the Homeland far from home..."

In an observation in which Gatto links the motives of warlike ancient Vikings with their longships to generations of transplanted sons and daughters in America, he comments:

"Is it so surprising that a cult of ships arose? Whatever pushed those beautiful craft night after night through mountainous seas to bloody wealth and fame became ideas and behaviors to revere. A man surviving and prospering by following the code of the longship would want his own sons to learn that code; others would speak of it in awe. When longships sailed no more the code was still taught: strength, youth, self-reliance, courage, exhilaration in the face of danger, contempt for weakness, keen watchfulness, mercilessness toward enemies, joy in treasure, *boredom with old planets, an appetite for new ones.*" [emphasis added]

Summing up ideas that seem to add up to a Junker *Alternative 3*, we are familiar with the advanced disk aircraft designs perfected by the Nazis during World War II, and also know that the American space program was run by prominent Nazis, or at least ex-Nazis. Nazi interests have also been entwined, since the emergence of the philosophy, with other totalitarian control mechanisms of the world, with the intelligence, police, and psychiatric establishments, with eugenics and genetic research, as well as with the plans of monied elites whose philosophies might better be defined in parapolitical, rather than political terms.

My belief is that the Nazis have been major, but far from the only players in the game of world domination since the end of World War II: one among many heads of the Hydra. Influential Nazis (possibly including Hitler) have been behind the scenes since the end of the war, creating and implementing schemes for the ultimate triumph of *Die Neuordnung*. Almost all of Hitler's cohorts survived Nuremberg and many have been involved in manipulations including international terrorism and the establishment of worldwide drug and arms markets, as well as in collaboration with other more "respectable" networks of world influence.

While I cannot state with certainty that Nazis are creating the "real" domination of *Alternative 3*, that they have constructed or are constructing bases on Mars or the moon to carry the ancient Grail of Aryan racial purity away from what they conceive as a cataclysm-doomed Earth, I do have to wonder at the logic and symmetry of detail.

21

Control

What is ultimately important about *Alternative 3* is not that it sets much of its grim script on the moon or Mars, or beneath "ice of Arctic" as Leslie Watkins says; those are merely locales that humans currently inhabit or will probably soon be erecting Golden Arches in. What is important is the explicit pointing to government and ruling class atrocity and human subjugation, and the warning it contains. *Alternative 3* is a scenario of the victimization of humankind — which I presume includes you — by power hungry men who have abandoned any consideration of morality or what is "right" and have replaced it with a mad "scientific" or philosophic lust for power. If you haven't gotten the idea that this world is run by a criminal elite lacking the slightest concern for the welfare of mankind, then you haven't been paying attention.

Alternative 3 points to, if in a clumsy and unbelievable fashion, the deadly alignment of technology and elitist control, and by exposing and calling attention to this collaboration, even in unintentional fashion as Watkins maintains happened, it is right on the mark.

I do not know whether all of the specific plans, the contingencies for 'batch consignments,' slave de-sexing, and interplanetary work camps exist in some policy letter, in the drawer of some Louis Quatorze desk in Geneva, or among some group of intelligence drones or clench of ruling elite. *Alternative 3* may not even be "true" at all, in the sense of the revealed scripture of some dark cabal, but only as a persuasive metaphor for totalitarian control in the manner of Orwell's *1984*.

I do know that, given the accelerating progression into dehumanizing and enslaving scientific technology and application that we have seen over the last one hundred years, given the move for greater police control and

the speedy erosion of our Constitutional, even human rights by governments elected and un-elected, that *Alternative 3*, in its worst and most grue-
some vision, is absolutely inevitable.

I have sifted clues in order to determine who the ultimate world conspirators are, and I believe that I have reached a workable plateau of understanding. While I am not saying that there might not exist one unifying
control structure overseeing secret societies and visible nation-states, that
there might not be a unifying capstone to the "pyramid" whose members
are pulling strings (and garottes) from behind the scenes, it is not necessary
to know the absolute identity of control in order to see how it works and to
recognize many of the leading players.

The summit of the pyramid consists of relatively tiny groups of aristocratic controlling families, exemplified by the powerful European and
American nodes of influence, the Rothschilds and the Rockefellers. Many
more of the most powerful "aristocratic" and "royal" families cluster
around these controllers, their members and influence richly deserving continued in-depth investigation. These families control and work in conjunction with secret societies such as the Knights of Malta, Freemasonry, the
Round Table, the Council on Foreign Relations, the Trilateral Commission,
the Bilderbergers, Skull and Bones and, judging from the prevalence of
New World Order themes in political manipulation, perhaps even the
Illuminati. Everything goes in shades, and some of the luminaries of these
societies have more knowledge and power than others. Other controlling
agencies include world intelligence organizations such as the CIA, KGB,
and British Intelligence, as well as international drug and terrorist networks
such as the Mafia and the extremely influential Nazi International, now
under a new generation of leadership that eschews swastika armbands. The
controllers, in their great wisdom, have displayed absolutely no qualms in
employing paid murderers, even genocide, to further their aims and to
maintain the structure of the pyramid.

Beneath the cloak of the prime conspirators are larger groups of rich
peasantry and landlords dominating a huge mass of poor serfs and less-
than-serfs whose labor and lives are sucked to provide the lifeblood to
nourish the upper portions of the pyramid. This ancient structure is perfectly visible to anyone with the eyes to be appalled. It is also obvious that
the ruling class cabals and spy organizations which we do know about are
pointed in roughly the same direction: the total control and "utilization" of
the mass of mankind by whatever means it takes.

Control is the shared goal of these numerous conspiring individuals,
groups, and governments, and in that sense they work together, collaborating here, working individually there, creating an evolving noose of murder-

ous technological expertise that swiftly tightens around humanity's throat. With this goal in place, with money and the tools of advanced technology in hand, the overall program of accomplishment crystallizes. It is sobering to note that with the advent of such technical innovations as DNA programming, mind control, robotics, and computer-biological interfacing, the statistically huge mass of "worker bees" are not only in danger, but also may be on the verge of becoming obsolete.

Researcher Hawthorne Abendsen has stimulated my thinking by suggesting that historical control may include a classified science of economic prediction that has been in operation for centuries. Prediction has long been the vocation of occultists and court astrologers who, far more likely than being engaged in creating individual sun sign charts, as Abendsen quips, were probably involved in the observance and anticipation of cyclic behavior in areas such as the weather, plagues and famines, war and market activity. I'm also reminded that as far back as the 1600s the Freemasons were reputed to possess "second sight," or the powers of ESP.

What we may be dealing with (at the level of the postulated masters of our masters) is an ancient system of hereditary wealth used in the financing of long term empirical observation, and the use of this wealth in accord with cyclic and social indicators, in promotion of the wars, the usurious credit systems, the technologies, and the pop-cultures, all ultimately engaged in the concentration of wealth into fewer and fewer hands.

In clear reflection of *Alternative 3*, this level of predictive technology might foresee environmental catastrophes far in advance of any science that we are familiar with, and have been preparing for such eventualities for far longer, even for centuries. The individuals utilizing this predictive technology may be promoting processes not unlike those described in *Alternative 3*, rendering humanity more and more tractable, more and more cattle-like, orchestrating the impersonal and harmonious dance of the hive in anticipation of their final flight from the planet.

It is possible that all of the generally accepted and cherished beliefs of mankind, the culture icons, the history, morals, religions, philosophies and even concepts are the carefully rehearsed theater of a cold-blooded ruling elite; illusory stage props in continual motion, and the means to parasitic ends. Trapping mankind in a haze of linguistic illusions and colored lights, in the Hollywood-like baffles of art, culture, patriotism, "lone nut" assassination, cataclysm and other spectacular gimmickry, these may be the means by which mankind's energies are manipulated and drained. Pondering the activities of mankind, including such relatively recent developments as mind control, fortified underground bases, genetic programming, and the invention of the means for space migration, I am chillingly reminded of the hive-programming of insects where masses of expendable and ignorant slave 'cells' are used for the pleasure and purposes of bloated kings, queens and their court.

Following a clue provided by Michael Hoffman II, I now see that any number of "insect" metaphors reside in the lore of governments and secret societies, with an emphasis on bees, according to Ordo Templi Orientis head Kenneth Grant a symbolic representation of a group mind proceeding from the "Queen" goddess Isis, beloved of the Freemasons and many another a mystical sect. Recalling the name of Illuminist Adam Weishaupt's secret society, the *Beenan Orden* (Order of the Bees), recalling the beehive emblem of the Freemasons and the Masonic offshoot Mormon Church's hive symbolism, I have to think that this must be a clue to the philosophy of these mystic Machiavellians.

A native/German sect in Colombia uses a swastika as icon and calls their compound "*Hormiga*," in honor of the ant, while the Sarmoung sect of the Sufis, reputed to have an unbroken lineage stretching back 2,000 years, call themselves "the Brotherhood of the Bee." This sect, interestingly enough, avows that their purpose is to halt the evolution of mankind, reserving the emergence of higher spiritual faculties and powers for an elect few.

Ernst Haeckel, Hitler's mentor in social Darwinism, thought that each cell of a living creature, "though autonomous, is subordinated to the body as a whole; in the same way in the societies of bees, ants, and termites, in the vertebrate herds, and in the human state, each individual is subordinate to the social body of which he is a member."

British author (and friend of Aldous Huxley) Gerald Heard in *Is Another World Watching?*, written in 1950, postulated at great length his "bee" theory of UFOs, suggesting these objects may represent the outward manifestation of an impersonal insectoid order run by a greater Overmind. And might there be humans who believe they represent this Overmind? Perhaps Heard is offering a clue when he muses about the Sphex wasp, "true mason wasp that it is."

Nesta Webster in *Secret Societies and Subversive Movements* wondered in 1924: "Has not the system of the ant-heap or the beehive proved... the model on which these modern Anarchists, from Proudhon onwards, have formed their schemes for the reorganization of human life? Has not the idea of the World State and The Universal Republic become the war-cry of the International Socialists, the Grand Orient Masons, Theosophists, and the world-revolutionaries of our own day?"

While I frankly don't believe that anarchists are the ones we need to fear, I take Webster's point and note that she is pointing to the forces that crystallized into the Round Table/Wall Street axis and the Nazis, among other groups. In short, the hive is the essence of the New World Order.

The insect metaphor resident in mystical literature is reminiscent of the basic elitist, anti-human theme of aristocratic "bluebloods" sustaining the hive through reproductive processes and blood lineage. It is even possible that the basic programming that controls mankind, both king and commoner, might be an instinctual ordering, an initiative encoded in DNA that captures us in designated castes, rather than plans written in some secret scroll and hidden in some secret vault.

And there may be a final secret to *Alternative 3*.

Scientists are currently engaged in research which may provide a powerful impetus for the elite of the world to plan ahead for off-world migration; that is the cracking of the code of aging. Michael West of the University of Texas Southwestern Medical Center in Dallas is only one among many researchers seeking answers to the reasons for aging. West, however, claims to have found those answers.

"We believe that cellular aging is the underlying mechanism of aging in the whole body," West says. "We have identified some of the genes activated during cellular aging, and we know the master switches that turn these genes on and off. We're making old cells young again in the laboratory. We're also able to change cells from a senescent state, in which they are no longer dividing, into an immortal one, in which they divide forever. And then we can reverse the process again, turning the dividing cells 'off.'"

West estimates that rejuvenation drugs based upon his research will be marketed in five to seven years, although he specifically disclaims that they will be "immortality drugs."

Is this the final vision of *Alternative 3*? Are we poised at the edge of the final sundering that Hitler envisioned, where immortal controllers assume complete control over the "bees of the hive"? Is that the ultimate rationale for the *Alternative 3* plan or a surrogate of it, that for the game to continue, everyone can't be a god?

It seems to me that, in order for complete control of mankind to be obtained by an elite or elites, be it military, political, philosophical, financial, or bloodline-based, then roughly the same reality-programs must be instituted.

It is necessary that any program of world domination to achieve total control must include broad psychological mastery over populations through propaganda, drugs, television, religion, or other mind control means. Physical control (consisting of hives, concentration camps, or contingency programs for same) must also be in place so that mass labor may be utilized in an economical fashion.

The control group should also have military strike capabilities for both offense and defense, preferably also possessing secret technology in advance of that of rival control factors.

Finally, plans for the preservation of the elite in the event of war, social upheaval, sudden recognition by the masses, or other catastrophe should be in place.

This broad outline of controls is a repetition, in almost all specifics, of the details of *Alternative 3*. It may also be an accurate reflection of the schemes of the shadow masters, judging historical events and ominous current indicators.

Ultimately the details hardly matter, because of the single conclusion which must be drawn. To the men who control this world (and their well-paid and smiling front men), we are all ultimately part of a 'batch consignment,' nothing more. And unless society is transformed from the inhuman control state we live in, unless the history of world domination is exposed and strategies for its elimination implemented, then the human race is doomed to live out this real world of *Alternative 3*.

Selected Bibliography

Allen, Gary. *None Dare Call It Conspiracy.* Concord Press, 1972

_____. *The Rockefeller File.* '76 Press, 1976

Anonymous. *Report From Iron Mountain on the Possibility and Desirability of Peace..* Dial Press, 1967

Baigent, Leigh and Lincoln. *Holy Blood, Holy Grail.* Dell Publishing Company, 1982

Baigent, Michael and Richard Leigh. *The Temple and the Lodge.* Arcade Publishing, 1989

Bamford, James. *The Puzzle Palace, A Report on America's Most Secret Agency.* Houghton Mifflin, 1982

Bower, Tom. *The Paperclip Conspiracy.* Little, Brown and Co., 1987

Brussel, Mae. *The Mae Brussell Reader.* Prevailing Winds, 1991

Garrison, Jim. *On the Trail of the Assassins.* Sheridan Square Press, 1988

Good, Timothy. *Above Top Secret: The Worldwide UFO Cover Up.* William Morrow & Company, 1988

Howard, Michael. *The Occult Conspiracy.* Destiny Books, 1989

Hunt, Linda. *Secret Agenda.* St. Martin's Press, 1991

Impact Team, The. *The Weather Conspiracy: The Coming of the New Ice Age.* Heron House Publishing International Ltd., 1977

Judge, John. *Judge For Yourself.* Prevailing Winds, 1991

Kasun, Jacqueline. *The War Against Population.* Ignatius Press, 1988

Kaysing, Bill. *We Never Went to the Moon.* Desert Publications, 1981

Kevles, Daniel J. *In the Name of Eugenics.* Alfred A. Knopf, 1985

Leary, Timothy. *Flashbacks.* J.P. Tarcher, Inc., 1983

McCoy, Alfred W. *The Politics of Heroin: CIA Complicity in the Global Drug Trade.* Harper & Row, 1991

Oppenheimer and Boyle. *Dead Heat, The Race Against the Greenhouse Effect.* Basic Books, Inc. 1990

Parfrey, Adam, ed. *Apocalypse Culture.* Feral House, 1991

Perloff, James. *The Shadows of Power: The Council on Foreign Relations and the American Decline.* Western Islands, 1988

Pool, James & Suzanne. *Who Financed Hitler, The Secret Funding of Hitler's Rise to Power 1919-1933.* Dial Press, 1978

Rifkin, Jeremy. *Biosphere Politics.* Crown Publishers, 1991

Sklar, Holly, ed. *Trilateralism.* South End Press, 1980

Skousen, W. Cleon. *The Naked Capitalist.* self published, 1970

Steckling, Fred. *We Discovered Alien Bases on the Moon.* GAF International Publishers, 1981

Stevenson, William. *The Bormann Brotherhood.* Harcourt, Brace, Jovanovich Inc., 1973

Sutton and Wood. *Trilaterals Over Washington.* The August Corporation, 1978

Sutton, Anthony. *Two Faces of George Bush.* Veritas Publishing Company Pty. Ltd., 1988

Tetens, T.H. *The New Germany and the Old Nazis.* Random House, 1961

Thomas, Gordon. *Journey into Madness, The True Story of Secret CIA Mind Control and Medical Abuse.* Bantam Books, 1989

Vankin, Jonathan. *Conspiracies, Cover-ups and Crimes.* Paragon House, 1992

Watkins, Leslie and David Ambrose. *Alternative 003* (in later editions *Alternative 3*). Sphere Books Ltd., 1978

Webster, Nesta. *Secret Societies and Subversive Movements.* Christian Book Club of America (first published in 1924)